# Women, Employment and Social Policy in Northern Ireland: a problem postponed?

Edited by:

## Celia Davies
## Eithne McLaughlin

*Publisher:*

Policy Research Institute
The Queen's University of Belfast
and the University of Ulster

*ISBN No.:*  **1 870654 11 0**

# CONTENTS

# EDITORS AND CONTRIBUTORS

## Editors

Celia Davies came to Northern Ireland in October 1987 to take up the newly created position of Professor of Women's Opportunities at the University of Ulster. She has been involved in the development of Women's Studies teaching and has established a Centre for Research on Women at the University. She is a sociologist with a research and publications record in equal opportunities for women and in the development of the professions, particularly the nursing profession.

Eithne McLaughlin has a doctorate in anthropology from The Queen's University of Belfast, and has held research posts in the Policy Research Institute, based in Coleraine, and, more recently, the Social Policy Research Unit at York. She is now a Lecturer in Women's Studies and Social Policy, a newly established post at Queen's University, Belfast. She has researched and published on gender, employment and unemployment, on social security, and on community care.

## Contributors

Eileen Evason is Senior Lecturer in Social Administration and Policy at the University of Ulster. She has carried out considerable research, written numerous pamphlets and articles on poverty, social security and women in Northern Ireland. She is a frequent broadcaster on these topics and is, among other things, active in the women's movement and the Child Poverty Action Group.

Bronagh Hinds is Area Director for Oxfam in Northern Ireland. She studied law at Queen's University, where she was the first woman president of the Students' Union. She has worked for a number of voluntary organisations and was Director of Gingerbread Northern Ireland for nine years. She has been a Commissioner on the Equal Opportunities Commission for Northern Ireland for eight years, is a past chairperson of the Northern Ireland Council for Voluntary Action, and is currently involved in the European Women's Lobby and the European Poverty Action Network.

Avila Kilmurray is a graduate of University College, Dublin, and has a MA in International Relations from The Australian National University. She has held a variety of posts including community worker in Derry, and Assistant Community Information Officer and later Development Officer with the Northern Ireland Council for Voluntary Action. In 1987, she was seconded to the Rural Action Project (NI), where she worked as co-ordinator until 1990. She is now the first Women's Officer in the Amalgamated Transport and General Workers Union in Northern Ireland.

Monica McWilliams is a Lecturer in Social Policy at the University of Ulster and is currently Senior Course Tutor for both graduate and non-graduate courses in Women's Studies. She has carried out work on family poverty and social deprivation at both the academic and community level in Northern Ireland. Her recent research has been on women in the labour market, and she is currently involved with women's groups in assessing the impact of "The Troubles" on their everyday lives in Northern Ireland.

Patricia Maxwell read law at the University of Bristol and now lectures in law at the University of Ulster. Her special interests include labour law, anti-discrimination law and health and safety at work. She has published in various journals and has worked with the Equal Opportunities Commission for Northern Ireland in an advisory capacity.

Pamela Montgomery has a doctorate in psychology from The Queen's University of Belfast. Her special areas of interest are violence against women, equal opportunities, women's employment and training. She co-authored a study of police response to wife assault, published by the Northern Ireland Women's Aid Federation. She was a Research Officer in the Centre for Research on Women at the University of Ulster and is now Chief Investigation Officer at the Equal Opportunities Commission for Northern Ireland.

Hazel Morrissey is a graduate of the University of Ulster, and works as a Research Officer for the Amalgamated Transport and General Workers Union. Her special areas of interest are the earnings structure in Northern Ireland, the new Fair Employment legislation, and the Single European Market and its effects on the Northern Ireland economy. She has been appointed to the new Fair Employment Tribunal, and she is also a member of her trade union's United Kingdom-wide Advisory Committee on Racial Equality.

# PREFACE

Books, like the people who write them, have a history that explains much of the form they take. The origins of this collection of essays lie in a series of meetings that took place between the editors early in 1988. One of us, newly arrived in Northern Ireland, with a daunting remit to develop teaching and research in women's studies at the University of Ulster, was searching for material, trying to build up a sense of what had been achieved and what now remained to be done. The other, then a Research Officer at the Policy Research Institute, with a working knowledge of what had been achieved, agreed that there was little available in a published and accessible form that would give a newcomer a sense of the strengths and weaknesses of this field of study in Northern Ireland.

From these discussions, more than one initiative took shape. Confidence grew in the concept of a Centre for Research on Women in Northern Ireland, something that was to begin to be put into place shortly thereafter; groundwork was laid for a bibliography of work on women's lives in Northern Ireland, which was subsequently completed in the new Centre; and, given the policy orientation of both of the editors, the idea of a series of public seminars on Women and Social Policy in Northern Ireland began to grow. The seminars were jointly sponsored by the Centre for Research on Women and the Policy Research Institute. The aim was to present recent work to a varied audience of academics, civil servants, politicians and other interested parties.

Four one-day seminars were held at Queen's University in Belfast on the topics of "Poverty and the Family", "Equality and the Work Environment", "Housing and the Environment", and "Law and the Family". Four or five papers were presented on each day, as were prepared comments from discussants. Attempts were made by the organisers and by those who chaired the sessions to provide summaries and overviews of the emerging themes. Participation had to be limited to 50, a limit that was reached, and even exceeded on occasions. This book represents a selection of the papers delivered at the first two of these seminars. Not all the papers could be included, and in no way should this volume be seen as a conference report. Six papers have been drawn directly from the presentations given, and one paper (by Pamela Montgomery), which was scheduled but had to be cancelled at the time, is now included.

As the seminar series developed, it began to confirm some of the points of our earlier discussions. Work on the position of women in Northern Ireland was not absent, but it was small scale, piecemeal, published often in ephemeral form or buried in books on other topics and thus not easy to locate. The Equal Opportunities Commission for Northern Ireland (EOCNI) had been important in developing and publishing a number of studies, and women's organisations, notably the Northern Ireland Women's Rights Movement, had initiated surveys and studies of specific topics. On the whole, however, the corpus of work on women available seemed not to be feeding into a policy debate in Northern Ireland, nor was it strongly affecting the teaching and research agendas of any but a small minority in the institutions of higher education.

The questions of why it is that women are off the policy agenda, how such a state of affairs is maintained, and how it could be changed, are posed in different ways by all the contributors to this book and taken up further in the concluding Chapter. For the first time for Northern Ireland, information about how women are treated in different policy areas is made available. In some policy areas, men and women are ostensibly treated equally, yet fare differently; in others, policy aimed directly at improving the lot of women has contradictory results. The contributions to this book should therefore be of interest to politicians, civil servants and trade unionists, as well as to students of social sciences and those taking a wide variety of women's studies courses.

If the book begins to involve a wider set of people, men as well as women, in the debate about what justice for women really entails and how greater equality between the sexes could be achieved in different policy areas, then it will have achieved its aim.

Celia Davies
Eithne McLaughlin

May, 1991

# ACKNOWLEDGEMENTS

The editors and contributors would like to thank all those who attended and participated in the original seminars, especially the chairpersons and discussants. The positive reaction to the seminar series persuaded us that the work we imposed on contributors, on ourselves and on those who helped to produce this volume would be worthwhile. The secretarial and indeed editorial work of Morag Stark was much appreciated, as was some important last-minute help from Pamela Montgomery. The final form of the book owes much to the professionalism with which Maura Carville carried out the last stages of preparation of the manuscript, and we are particularly grateful to her for this.

# CHAPTER ONE

# INTRODUCTION: A PROBLEM POSTPONED

## EITHNE McLAUGHLIN

This book is about women in Northern Ireland, and, in particular, about the way women's socio-economic position is created or maintained by public policy. The book is about fundamentals - it is about how the work and time of women is valued and rewarded. "Work" here is used in its broadest sense to mean the expenditure of mental or physical effort to a purpose. This means the book is about the nature and level of the return women get, individually and collectively, for their participation in society. That participation takes many shapes and forms - ranging from paid work of greater or lesser degrees of formality, to unpaid work, caring for young, old and disabled others, and producing and consuming home commodities. In all these areas, the participation of men and women differs from each other and is differently rewarded.

Although many of the Chapters in this book seem to take as their focus women's participation in, access to and reward for, paid work, it is, in fact, the interface between paid and unpaid work, between the labour market and the rest of the social world, which is analysed and commented on in each case. Because the family, the market and the State are not distinct spheres of human activity, a book on "social" policy has also to be a book on "economic" policy. Indeed the division between "the social" and "the economic", like that between "the public" and "the private", serves to obscure the relationship between paid and unpaid work and that between the State and the individual. It is, however, only by developing analyses which cross these divides that we can understand the nature, purpose and impact of state intervention in the lives of individuals in society (and hence the meaning of "citizenship" and "participation").

In doing so, we inevitably expose and confront major differences in the way the State relates to men and women. But the issues thus raised are still inadequately recognised (if recognised at all) by the majority of policy analysts and policy-makers, in Great Britain and, more especially, in Northern Ireland. All the contributors to this book ask, in their different ways, why this should be so. Their answers have fed from, and been informed by, the activities of feminist scholars in the academic field of social policy since the early 1970s and it is to these we now turn.

## Social Policy and Inequality

Social policy has been traditionally concerned with examination of the extent and causes of inequality between individuals, categories of individuals, and social groups in society. And, following from that, with an evaluation of the role of existing social and economic policies in creating, perpetuating or reducing those inequalities. Whether reduction of social and economic inequality is a desirable goal, and, if it is desirable, the degree of reduction desirable, is one key debate in social policy. The directions which future policy would need to take in order to achieve the desired level of reduction of inequality is another.

As a discipline, therefore, social policy has spanned economics, sociology and social anthropology on the one hand and philosophy and political science on the other. Three major schools of thought can be identified in the discipline, each associated with a closely related political philosophy: anti-collectivism (the New Right); mainstream social reformism (various hues of the left); and the political economy of welfare (Marxist and neo-Marxist) (See Williams, 1989). By far the most dominant school both in Great Britain and Northern Ireland has been social reformism which covers a wide spectrum from non-socialist welfare collectivism (welfare pluralism) through Fabian socialist traditions to radical social administration. These traditions have focused on social divisions between rich and poor and have provided extensive analyses of poverty, redistribution and the social division of welfare.

Class analysis of one kind or another has provided the major point of reference for the studies of social inequality that lie at the heart of social policy. Fiona Williams (1989) has documented in some detail how feminist and Black theories and critiques of the welfare state in the 1970s and 1980s, have challenged existing academic traditions. Fabian socialism has met the challenges of ethnicity and gender by focusing on the denial of existing citizenship rights to these categories caused by ''discrimination'', in turn caused by ''social custom, values and prejudices''. These, it is argued, can be modified by legal and educational change (Glennerster, 1983). This academic response dovetails neatly with State responses to evidence of pervasive inequality between Blacks and Whites in Great Britain, Protestants and Catholics in Northern Ireland, and men and women in both. In each case, it has taken the form of the development of anti-discrimination legislation, allocating the accompanying tasks of education and enforcement to specialised, semi-autonomous agencies - the Commission for Racial Equality (CRE) and the Equal Opportunities Commission (EOC) in Great Britain, the Equal Opportunities Commission for Northern Ireland (EOCNI) and the Fair Employment Agency (FEA) (more recently, the Fair Employment Commission), in Northern Ireland.

Growing evidence in the 1980s that anti-discrimination measures have achieved a limited amount in terms of reducing inequality has fed into a more radical school of social reformism which draws on the empiricism of Fabianism and the structuralism of Marxism (See, for example, Townsend, 1979, 1984; Walker, 1982, 1984; Mishra, 1986). The result is an acknowledgement that sexism, along with racism and sectarianism, are institutionalised, structural problems in society but with singularly little success in offering policy directions which actually deal with the problems. A similar process has arisen within the political economy of welfare tradition - gender and ethnicity have been acknowledged to be structurally important, but in this case remain theoretically subordinated to the structural opposition of classes. As Williams (1989) has pointed out, analyses based on the concept of class struggle in the production of "work" and "welfare" imply a unity of classes which fails to address the historical evidence that gains for some sections of classes can be losses for other sections of the same class. Existing traditions of scholarship within social policy have therefore tended to emphasise one type of inequality to the exclusion or minimisation of others.

Meanwhile, a body of critical work on social policy and its implications for women has been steadily growing (See for example, Dale and Foster 1986, Pascall 1986). This work has been concerned with "mainstream" topics such as poverty and the family (Glendinning and Millar, 1987), unemployment (Cragg and Dawson, 1984), health (Graham, 1984) as well as with "new" topics such as domestic violence (Hanmer and Maynard, 1987; Kelly, 1988). These topics have been examined from the standpoint of women, examined in such a way that new conceptualisations, new questions and new stances on policy have emerged. The recognition, present but unheeded at the time when Beveridge was at work fashioning the postwar welfare state, that its very design would underline a different basis of citizenship for women, deepening their reliance on men and reinforcing their dependency (Abbot and Bompas, 1943), has proved to be the touchstone of work on women and social policy in the 1980s.

This work repeatedly draws attention to the structural principles which underpin women's dependency and the ideological supports which construct a "private sphere" where policy is reluctant to intervene and which applauds, and at the same time ignores for policy purposes, the caring work (low paid and unpaid) that women do.

Such new work is being complemented in two ways. First, and not unexpectedly it is within socialist feminism and Black Feminism in Great Britain that attempts to understand the interlocution of class, gender and ethnicity have been moving forward. Walby (1986, 1990), for example, has been attempting on the one hand, theoretically to acknowledge the significance of institutionalised power relationships between men and women which produce gender inequalities and on the other, to acknowledge that capitalism gives rise to differential experiences of oppression by women of different classes. Bhavanani and Coulson (1986) have suggested that feminism has to recognise that the State deals with different women differently and that there may be different strategies for black women and white women, strategies which emerge from "the interweaving of patriarchy, imperialism and capitalism" and which in turn serve to structure women's experience as different (Williams 1989, p 86). Secondly, there are more direct efforts to promote a reframing of policy to account for the growing understanding of women's structured dependency. Critiques of discrimination legislation and of measures insisting on identical treatment of the two sexes fit into this category (Gregory, 1987; Lacey, 1987; Davies, 1989), so too does the debate about recasting citizenship rights (See for example, Lister, 1990), something that could well be seen as underlying the arguments of many of the Chapters in this volume. This thinking, which owes much to the intellectual energy of feminism in the 1980s, sits uneasily with the marriage of mainstream social reformism and government policy responses which was noted earlier and thus far at any rate, has not been acknowledged or incorporated either into policy practice or intellectual debate. It is in this sense, that the question of women and social policy in Great Britain as well as in Northern Ireland, may be said to be a problem postponed.

## Social Policy in Northern Ireland

In practical terms, much of public policy in Northern Ireland since 1972 has been informed by explicit adherence to two principles - firstly that of being seen to do something about the Northern Ireland problem (that is, "sectarian" conflict) and secondly that of securing parity of provision with that in Great Britain. As Osborne and Cormack (1989) have suggested, these two principles do not necessarily sit easily together. Failures to achieve even formal parity in some areas - for example in law enforcement - are expressed as unfortunate by-products of "The Troubles", while unwillingness to intervene beyond a certain level in Northern Ireland's economic and social problems is expressed in terms of the undesirability of breaking parity of treatment between Northern Ireland and Great Britain (for example, in relation to regional economic policy, gender inequality, and social security (See Bradshaw 1989)). Both issues have served to shape academic enquiry into social policy in Northern Ireland, and both, in their different ways have helped to postpone questions of the implications of policy for women.

The "Northern Ireland problem" as it is commonly understood is one of violent sectarianism and inequality between Catholics and Protestants. Both the State and the media have defined "the problem" in these terms and such definitions have permeated the social science academic world too - structured as it is by the availability of research funding for the investigation of "social problems". This is not to say that academics have not endeavoured to raise the profile of Northern Ireland's "other" problems. They have - and these have been seen as problems of depressed economic activity, poverty and unemployment. Indeed, the most vibrant debates have been around the interaction of Catholic/Protestant inequality and poverty and unemployment, and the question of which is the most "important" or "prior" inequality. The past, and continuing, centrality of Catholic/Protestant relations in policy and research has obscured the realities of other forms of inequality to varying degrees, with gender inequality very low on the list. Just as importantly, it has obscured the overlaps, interaction and interlocution of key forms of inequality - religious/political, gender, spatial and class.

The parity problem constantly pushes the comparative gaze towards Great Britain. One result is that the differential impact of economic and social policies on different geographical areas of Northern Ireland, and on different social groups and categories within Northern Ireland, has received little attention. That is, discussion of parity of outcome for rural versus urban dwellers, women versus men, west versus east, and so on, has been stifled under the blanket of parity between Northern Ireland and Great Britain. Yet the size of intra-Northern Ireland difference is in many instances greater than that between Northern Ireland and Great Britain and particularly that between areas of Northern Ireland and subregional areas of Great Britain (See Ditch and Morrissey, 1989; Gaffikin and Morrissey, 1990).

Unemployment is a case in point. The difference between the unemployment rates of East and West in Northern Ireland is roughly the same as the difference between the unemployment rate of Northern Ireland and Great Britain and certainly greater than the difference between the unemployment rates of Northern Ireland and other depressed regions and areas of Great Britain. The experience of economic disadvantage is not, therefore, a uniformly Northern Ireland-wide one and, as Ditch and Morrissey have commented, the notion that Northern Ireland as a whole is a "depressed region" is imprecise (Ditch and Morrissey, 1989, p 7). Inequalities are specifically located among certain social groups and categories, and although the "rules" by which economic disadvantage and inequality are transmitted are complex, it is clear that gender is one such highly significant "structuring" factor.

All of this means that the picture of women's lives is particularly hard to piece together since priorities have been elsewhere. It does not, however, mean that there is an absence of such material altogether, as the following section shows.

## Women in Northern Ireland

The centrality of Catholic-Protestant relations in policy and research has led to an accepted wisdom that women in Northern Ireland are particularly oppressed by the influence of conservative religious ideologies and by the parochial or inward-looking nature of life in a divided and troubled society. Linda Edgerton, for example has commented:

> Given the bitter political divisions of Northern Ireland, its depressed socio-economic conditions and the powerfully conservative influence of the dominant churches, it is little wonder that women have remained in a relative backwater of feminism. (Edgerton, 1986, p 61)

She goes on to suggest further underpinnings of women's oppression that lie in family structures and networks in Northern Ireland:

> in many working-class communities the extended family network has not only remained but been reinforced by the "troubles" [providing] a further barrier to the development of female independence...The men in the family along with their male friends form a close-knit group which serves to reinforce each

other's ideas, prejudices and stereotypes. The women, on the other hand, are not guaranteed support from female relatives if they are viewed as flouting the community norms and conventions influenced by the local churches. (Edgerton, 1986, p 81)

Analysis of women's roles in other pluralist and conflict-ridden societies (See Ridd and Calloway, 1986) suggest that in such contexts gender polarity is often promoted in order to assert cultural identity:

> Aligned with this heightened ideology of gender difference another factor comes into play during a time of conflict. To strengthen group mobilisation, cultural or class identity often becomes "tradition" - that cultural storehouse of historical events, mythical happenings, evocative symbols and elusive images which can be used to convey charged meaning in the present. (Calloway, 1986, p 228)

The recent work of Chavetz, attempting to theorise the conditions under which moves to greater gender equity occur, and drawing on a wide range of cross cultural examples, also points to links between internal conflict and heightened traditionalism in women's roles (Chavetz, 1990, p 119-121). Studies have also documented more specifically in Northern Ireland the way that women's participation in the political arena has been seen as, and expressed as, an extension of their traditional maternal role as "guardian of the family" and women activists have been dubbed "family feminists" in this respect (Mitchison, 1988; cf Edgerton, 1986). Yet the process by which political activity by women is "made safe" has not been without its own contradictions and tensions. There is a growing divergence of views within Nationalist and Republican traditions, in particular, between those who emphasise women's family roles (Mother Ireland) and those who argue that Ireland cannot be "free" until women are "free". The former view is well expressed in a *Cumann na mBan* statement quoted in Ward:

> We see our role in society as equal to men's, though naturally not the same, and it will be towards the fulfilment of womanhood and the acceptance of the value of women in society that we will strive...We see ourselves as the women of Ireland, the mothers of future generations of Irish men and women and we consider this no mean role in life. We consider the family as the basic unit of society and it is as the defenders of all that is good in society that we have acted. (1984, p 261)

Sinn Fein policy documents since 1980 have, however, represented somewhat uneasy attempts to balance these two opposing forces within Republicanism and accounts of a number of recent feminist struggles show a more complex picture than "family feminism" would imply (Devaney et al, 1989).

Against such pictures of repressed, conservative and dominated women, has to be set the not inconsiderable level of women's activity in women's organisations such as the Northern Ireland Women's Rights Movement (set up in 1975) and Northern Ireland Women's Aid. Whether the level of such activity is lower than that to be found in other areas of the United Kingdom cannot be ascertained without comparative research with a United Kingdom area of similar population size. The level of activity does not however appear *prima facie* to be low given the size of Northern Ireland (1.5 million).

There is also evidence from within this volume and elsewhere (See for example, Trewsdale, 1988 and McShane and Pinkerton, 1986) that women's lives in Northern Ireland have changed substantially since the 1960s. During the 1960s, women's participation in paid employment, and particularly the participation of married women, increased enormously. In 1961, only 30 per cent of female employees were married; by 1971, nearly half were married (47 per cent); and in the 1980s, the majority of women in paid employment were married - 59 per cent in 1981 (Northern Ireland Census of Population, Economic Activity Tables, 1961, 1971, 1981). The 1970s brought important reductions in fertility rates and family size so that by the late 1980s, the live birth rate was 17.7 in Northern Ireland compared with 13.6 in the United Kingdom as a whole (Regional Trends, 1989) and the average number of children, 2.2 (Policy, Planning and Research Unit, (PPRU) Monitor, No 3/89).

The 1980s have also been characterised by a doubling of the number of births occurring outside marriage and large increases in the proportions of lone parent families. By 1988, 16 per cent of all births were births outside marriage (PPRU, 1989) compared with seven per cent in 1981 and only four per cent in 1971. Likewise, in 1988, 16 per cent of families with dependant children were headed by a lone mother and two per cent by a lone father (*ibid*). There has been a rapid increase ever since the mid 1980s when ten per cent of families were headed by a lonemother and two per cent by lone fathers (McShane and Pinkerton, 1986). Both the direction of change in all these areas of social and economic life, and the rate of change, in the 1960s, 1970s and 1980s, has been the same in Northern Ireland as in Great Britain. Whether, in this context, Northern Ireland is indeed hallmarked by particularly "traditional" and rigid cultural and economic gender roles must be a matter not for speculation but for empirical investigation which takes these trends, as well as other matters, into account. The role of "The Troubles" in constraining women's lives in Northern Ireland also requires careful and detailed research. There are a number of dimensions here to take into account. While, in international terms, the level of conflict is low when measured in terms of violent deaths (Ditch and Morrissey, 1989 p 20), the less direct effects of "The Troubles" are also important. The lives of women can be affected considerably, by for example, the 1971 Payment for Debt (Emergency Provisions) Act (NI), which was introduced in response to the political protest rent and rates strike of the early 1970s. The widely used provisions of this Act (See for example, Evason 1980, 1986, 1987) permit public bodies to make direct deductions at source from social security benefits, or earnings if the debtor is employed by central or local government or public utilities. There are also the special dimensions domestic and sexual violence may take on in such a context. Evason (1982) has identified men's access to firearms, the protection of an abusing man through his membership of paramilitary or military organisations and community bias against calling on police assistance in Nationalist areas as factors increasing women's vulnerability. Then there is the effect of "The Troubles" on apparently unrelated policy measures dealing with employment and unemployment.

A good example here is Rees' analysis of special employment and training measures for young people. This showed that girls in Northern Ireland were offered fewer, cheaper and poorer quality placements than boys. Whilst Northern Ireland is not exceptional in its sex-stereotypical provision of training and work experience to young women, she argues that concern for this is "over-shadowed by the political need to be seen to be carrying out effective policies geared towards the reform of sectarianism" (Rees, 1983 p 168). Under Direct Rule, there is no doubt that there has been considerable effort given to being seen to be "doing something" about Catholic/Protestant inequality. External pressure from America has had its effect in the recent (1988) strengthening of anti-religious discrimination law and policy in Northern Ireland.

> This owes much to the international context of the Northern Ireland problem and relatively little to [a Conservative Government's] commitment to promoting equal opportunities. As the Northern Ireland proposals took shape the phrase most often to be heard from civil servants was "the problem of

read-across", by which was meant the extreme sensitivity felt
by the government to the argument that if such a strengthened
policy could be promoted in Northern Ireland then why not in
the rest of the United Kingdom?  By confining the new policy
to religion (and not gender and disability) it could be depicted
as of relevance only to Northern Ireland - "a place apart".
(Osborne and Cormack, 1989 p 293)

## Northern Ireland's "Problem Postponed"

There are two conflicting positions that might be put concerning women
and social policy in Northern Ireland today.  The one, drawing on a thesis
of traditionalism, would be inclined to say that the pattern of female
dependency assumed in the welfare state measures of the 1940s remains
a better fit for the Northern Ireland than the British case, and from that
point of view, the case for change is not an urgent one.  The other,
diametrically opposed, would claim that, when given the opportunity, women
participate in the labour market, and that they are already doing so in
increasing proportions and for an increasing amount of their total life span.
From this, the argument might go on to claim that any special consideration for women is misplaced in face of the need to improve the Northern
Ireland economy generally.

Chapter Two by Monica McWilliams shows that both perspectives
are far from accurate.  By taking three existing survey sources and linking
these with other data, published and unpublished, she is able to pose a
wide range of questions concerning married women's participation in the
labour market, its determinants and consequences.  In doing so, she provides
an array of important findings which we need to assimilate and evaluate
as a prelude to the development of socio-economic policies which will
benefit women.

The male breadwinner pattern, as she clearly demonstrates, is still
important but is no longer, even in "traditional" Northern Ireland, the
dominant pattern.  Instead, it is dual earner couples that are most prevalent.  Households in which neither partner earns income are also important
for Northern Ireland.  The decision processes that lead to women's participation in employment are complex ones, governed not only by the jobs on
offer, but by the hours available and unshared responsibility for childcare.
From the kind of evidence McWilliams is able to adduce, it may well be
that material conditions are more important in the end than are assumptions about the traditional attitudes (of women, men or both) in Northern

Ireland. Certainly in drawing attention to the comparatively high figure of 50 per cent of married women who record themselves as "keeping house", she is able effectively to criticise those who say this is caused by Northern Ireland's "traditionalism" and that that is the end of the matter.

The data base from which McWilliams is working, as she herself points out, is far from ideal for her purpose. She has to leave open, for example, the question of women's income contribution to the household, notwithstanding its obvious relevance to her theme. She also, in the confines of a short Chapter, has to be selective. The absence of published commentary on women's employment in Northern Ireland is striking. The EOCNI commissioned work some years ago for a series of *"Woman-power"* reports. Individual academics have also published accounts from time to time (Ditch and Osborne, 1980; Aunger, 1983; Trewsdale, 1983). No government source to date has published any such review, a startling omission given the patterns which this Chapter reveals.

McWilliams' Chapter demonstrates the complex interaction between women's unpaid work and their labour force participation. It also highlights the dynamic relationship between husbands' and wives' unemployment and non-employment, which in turn leads to different outcomes for Catholic and Protestant families. In Chapter Three, Hazel Morrissey deals with yet further complicated interactions. Women's responsibility for unpaid as well as paid work leads to lower pay for women relative to men; but her Chapter also brings to the fore the interaction of class and gender, resulting in different outcomes for working-class and middle-class women. The main focus of Morrissey's Chapter is on comparisons of pay - comparisons between men and women, between manual and non-manual women and between Great Britain and Northern Ireland.

Drawing from the most recently available data from the *New Earnings Survey*, Morrissey emphasises the growing earnings gap between those doing manual and those doing non-manual work. There is widening inequality in earnings for men as well as for women, and the pay gap between the highest and lowest earners for each sex has grown wider in recent years. Furthermore, not only are manual women workers worse off than their non-manual equivalents within Northern Ireland but they are also worse off than their manual equivalents in Great Britain - a difference between Northern Ireland and Great Britain which does not apply to non-manual women. Manual women workers have also seen a real decrease in their earnings since 1987, whereas non-manual women workers have not. More work needs to be done both on the determinants of women's low pay in Northern Ireland and on the consequences of it for them and their families.

Morrissey provides a pioneering discussion in this context of the likely effects of the Single European Act on working women in Northern Ireland.  For some, she argues, particularly those who are already in positions of high pay and status, change will bring new prospects and new horizons. For the unskilled and low paid, the prospects are bleak and include the reinforcement of women's dependency and inequality.  Like several of the contributors, she looks to European Directives for the specification and enhancement of women's rights in relation to employment, and she provides a valuable update on the range of measures currently under discussion.

Morrissey's and McWilliams' Chapters on low pay and levels of participation, respectively, prepare the ground for Chapter Four by Eileen Evason on women and poverty. This Chapter is of a different kind.  Evason examines the consequences of women's responsibility for both paid and unpaid work for their entitlement (or lack of it) to material rewards commensurate with those of men.  The level of reward women receive for their labours is undoubtedly low.  Rather than attempting to measure women's poverty on the basis of inadequate statistical information, her contribution is to outline the need for a complete rethinking of the notion of poverty itself; this is a call, as her Chapter makes clear, that is growing ever more insistent as both the poverty lobby and academics begin to take women into account.

Taking women into account in discussing poverty means acknowledging that married women have no right to maintenance as such, and recognising that the law does not insist on the pooling of household resources. Without earnings in their own right or earnings of a high enough level, therefore, women's access to resources, as Evason says, is always indirect and at the discretion of another.  This is why, when women become single parents, and in receipt of benefit directly instead of managers of an income given them at the discretion of their husbands, they often report that they are "better off".  What then happens when we try to estimate the numbers of women who have direct access to a reasonable income of some kind? Adding together married women who are not working, employed women of whatever marital status who can be regarded as low-paid, and single women living on benefits serves to account for fully three-quarters of the adult female population in Northern Ireland.  We can, of course, debate whether we would want to describe all these women as living in poverty. Undoubtedly, however, they do share a position of disadvantage as far as independent access to material resources is concerned. And that lack of independent access in turn undoubtedly contributes to dependency, powerlessness and hence inequality, in both a subjective and an objective sense.

Evason calls for a wide array of policy changes, changes designed to tackle low pay and unpaid work as well as changes in the system of social security itself. Her notion of a "principle of equal concern" in relation to social security provision is an important one, but equally important is her insistence that we consider the wider framework of contemporary change in the welfare state, change which, in areas other than those considered in this volume (health for example) is predicated on the continuing availability of women for unpaid labour.

Taken together, Chapters Two - Four underline the marked differences in women's labour market position in relation to men and in women's command over material resources of all kinds. All this is to suggest not that women simply prefer not to participate in paid work (though some clearly do), but that access to paid employment is structured in such a way that few women can earn sufficient for themselves, or for themselves and a family. We must not lose sight of the vulnerability that this labour market position brings, in terms of a sexual division of labour in the home, in terms of expectations about childcare, domestic work in the home, opportunities, or the lack of them, to leave an unhappy marriage, and opportunities, or the lack of them, to commence or restart a career at midlife. And we must ask whether it is not time to change social and economic policies which limit women's choices in this way.

The next Chapter turns to the fate of recent legislation on equal pay in Northern Ireland. This is an area where policy is directed specifically towards the amelioration of women's disadvantage, and where, on the face of it, one would expect the record to be an encouraging one. A view, however, that the legislation is tortuous, complex and ambiguous is shared by the legal profession and the lay public. Patricia Maxwell (Chapter Five) reviews the relatively new provisions for equal pay for work of equal value, developed following a ruling by the European Court of Justice in 1982. The central idea - that someone can judge whether one person's work is equal in value to another's - is fraught with difficulty. The potentially different considerations that the "independent expert" in these cases might apply, compared to those applied by conventional job evaluators, are proving contentious. Even where the independent expert succeeds in producing an assessment of value of the different jobs in question, it is not at all clear what the legal status of such findings is. Furthermore, the equal value amendment has not overcome the problem of occupational segregation. A woman must use a male comparator employed by the same employer and employed within Northern Ireland. Because of high levels of vertical as well as horizontal segregation, this will be difficult for many women workers in Northern Ireland.

The analysis of cases in progress that Maxwell provides and her commentary on them raises a number of important questions about the conditions for policy success. How far are the procedural difficulties a function of the lack of government commitment in this area - how far do they represent a missed opportunity on the part of the judiciary? Where do the employers and the trade unions stand? What should never be forgotten is the courage that it takes for an individual woman to take a case, the dangers of demoralisation and victimisation which she may then suffer. Here, and in relation to discrimination legislation more generally, the assumption is that the basic system is a fair one, and that it is only in exceptional instances that action is needed. To the extent that this is untrue, to the extent that women's disadvantage is structural, such legislation will always be unwieldy and will always mean that individual women will bear a high personal cost of attempted change.

The remaining Chapters turn attention to specific areas where policy development, in principle at least, could be of strategic importance in recognising the structured disadvantage women face and in beginning to ensure more equal rewards for the labour (paid and unpaid) of women and men. We start with the unshared nature of childcare in Northern Ireland. Bronagh Hinds (Chapter Six) draws both from her experience in campaigning for childcare and from findings of a recently published study of childcare in the European Community to piece together the pattern of current provision and policy development in this area in Northern Ireland. The overall picture is a sorry one from the point of view of those who would want to see some sharing of responsibilities for childcare between the State and individual women. Not only is the level of statutory childcare provision in Northern Ireland very much lower than that in Great Britain (this being one area where the principle of parity in any sense of the term has never been applied), but also, from a Europe-wide perspective, United Kingdom support for childcare, and for other measures such as maternity provision, is near the bottom of the league. A useful account of the history and current level of provision is followed by an analysis of the published policy of the four Health and Social Service Boards in Northern Ireland. It is, as Hinds points out, quite understandable that local authority policy should be interpreted within the legal framework offered by central government. The net result, however, is a narrowly focused set of provisions, targeted on "problem families" and "at risk" children, all a far cry from a universal service responding to the needs of children on the one hand and working parents on the other. The contradictions of such an approach at a time when women, in Great Britain at least, are being encouraged to return to the labour market are all too apparent.

Training policy, in the specific case considered here of youth training, is a different matter. Policy and provision is avowedly universal, it is designed to offer young people (girls as well as boys) a route to acquisition of the skills and competencies that will equip them for a place in the labour market consistent with their abilities and aspirations. Such training should offer young women a route out of the segregated labour market and an opportunity to focus their ambitions on jobs with greater prospects.

Pamela Montgomery (Chapter Seven) gives an account of a recent study of the operation of the Youth Training Programme and of the facilities it is providing to widen the horizons of young women at the point of their entry to the labour market. Many of those involved in the scheme, as she shows, argue that this is a point where males and females start from an equal footing and where they are offered a genuine and free choice. If girls and boys make different choices, and a glance at the overall statistics or a visit to almost any scheme in operation shows that they do, there is little in the view of the staff that they themselves could or should do about it. The Chapter offers a closely observed account of how interpretations of *de facto* sex segregation differ, but how in the end inaction is justified. It also documents some of the reactions of the girls and boys themselves.

There is, as Montgomery points out, a considerable amount of research to show how, at home and at school, young women's horizons have been limited as far as aspirations for employment are concerned even before they reach a training scheme. There is also a recognition, more among the girls and boys themselves, and less among the staff, of the hassle and harrassment that girls will face if they attempt to train in a non-traditional area. Where this is recognised, instead of asking how girls' needs can be accommodated, staff look for the "super-girl", the one who can succeed against the odds. Here, as in the case of the equal value legislation, is a piece of policy provision which, on paper, looks as if it could benefit women. But those who operate a policy may fail to see, or fail to agree with, its equal opportunity implications, and where this is the case, it is unlikely to have its intended outcomes.

Failure to see women, to recognise women's needs and to use the contributions that women have to offer are all themes of Avila Kilmurray's Chapter on rural development (Chapter Eight).  The Rural Action Project, a four-year programme of action research funded by the second European Commission Anti-Poverty Programme, has already brought policy-makers and rural dwellers together and generated considerable interest in strategies for the future.  Based on a survey of women in South Armagh, this Chapter gives important glimpses of the material conditions of women's lives in rural areas and of the needs and aspirations they express.  The very different lives of women in rural and urban areas, and the different meanings and consequences of paid and unpaid labour in each, have not previously been the focus of much attention in Northern Ireland.  Here, Avila Kilmurray begins to draw out these differences.

The absence of an adequate infrastructure, in the shape of good public transport facilities, as Kilmurray shows, has a marked effect on the quality of women's lives in rural areas, especially when they are trying to juggle childcare, care of other dependents, housework and work on a farm. The net result can be be a logistical nightmare and a real sense of isolation.  Women in paid work present a familiar picture of service sector, low-paid employment and of difficulties in arranging childcare.  All this is compounded by the limited number of job opportunities in areas such as in South Armagh and by transport problems.  What then of their aspirations? While Kilmurray talks of rural traditionalism, she also finds strong generational effects which cry out for further study.  Thus, while older women were more doubtful, approaching half of the women with young children approved of women working if the opportunities presented themselves, and three-quarters of a sample of schoolgirls said the same.

Women have ideas.   The development of tourism, agricultural diversification, self-help enterprises and cottage industries were on their lists for regeneration of the area.  Yet women are also torn.  Many of them saw unemployment first and foremost as a male problem or a problem for young people rather than a priority for (adult) women.  On the other hand, as Kilmurray points out, women are already making an important contribution to the survival of an area to which they are highly committed.  Any new strategy must ensure that women's needs are articulated and women's contribution, both currently and potentially, can be taken into account. The Council of Europe Conference approach as described by Avila Kilmurray has much to commend it, and far from constraining policy development, the further integration of women into the policy process could serve to widen the range of possibilities.

Each of the Chapters in the main body of this book has suggestions for policy development, suggestions which are sometimes presented in considerable detail. What are the prospects for change? The final Chapter (Chapter Nine) takes a critical look at the current climate and at the array of forces to be considered. Whether, in the end, that analysis proves to be correct, the overwhelming evidence of gender inequality, and the dismissal of that inequality from the policy agenda in Northern Ireland, presented in these Chapters remains a key feature of social and economic life in Northern Ireland today. The lack of attention paid by academics and policy-makers to that inequality has been justified on the grounds that Northern Ireland has more "pressing" problems. But gender inequality cannot be separated from these "other" problems. Male and female employment and unemployment interact dynamically; the economic disadvantage of women, through low pay, the direct and indirect effects of the benefit system, and the unrewarded nature of so much of women's work, is a key cause of household poverty in Northern Ireland; and not all women are equally disadvantaged or disadvantaged in the same ways. Gender inequality cannot be separated from other forms of inequality in Northern Ireland - and it is a problem that should no longer be postponed.

# REFERENCES

ABBOT E. and BOMPAS K., (1943) *The Woman Citizen and Social Security*, London: Katherine Bompas

AUNGER E. A., (1983) "Religion and Class: an analysis of 1971 Census Data" in R. J. Cormack and R. D. Osborne (Eds), *Religion, Education and Employment: Aspects of Inequality in Northern Ireland*, Belfast: Appletree Press

BHAVANANI K. and COULSON, M., (1986) "Transforming Socialist - Feminism: the Challenge of Racism", *Feminist Review*, 23

BRADSHAW J., (1989) *Social Security Parity in Northern Ireland*, Occasional Paper, Belfast: Policy Research Institute

CALLOWAY H., (1986) "Survival and Support: Women's Forms of Political Action" in R. Ridd and H. Calloway (Eds), *Caught up in Conflict: Women's Responses to Political Strife*, London: Macmillan

CHAVETZ J. S., (1990) *Gender Equity*, London: Sage

COMPTON P. and COWARD J., (1989) *Fertility and Family Planning in Northern Ireland*, Aldershot: Avebury

CRAGG A. and DAWSON T., (1984) *Unemployed Women: a Study of Attitudes and Experiences*, London: Department of Employment, Research Paper No 47

DALE J. and FOSTER P., (1986) *Feminists and State Welfare*, London Routledge and Kegan Paul

DAVIES C., (1989) "Workplace Action Programmes for Equality for Women: An Orthodoxy Examined", in C. Hussey (Ed), *Equal Opportunities for Men and Women in Higher Education in Ireland*, (conference proceedings), Dublin: University College Dublin

DEVANEY F., MULHOLLAND M. and WILLOUGHY J., (1989) (Eds)*Unfinished Revolution: Essays on the Irish Women's Movement*, Belfast: Meadbh Publishing

DITCH J. and MORRISSEY M., (1989) "Northern Ireland 1979-1989: Review and Prospects for Social Policy", paper delivered to the SPA Conference: Bath, July

DITCH J. and OSBORNE R., (1980) *Women and Work in Northern Ireland: A Survey of Data*, Jordanstown, Co Antrim: Ulster Polytechnic School of Sociology and Social Policy, Occasional Paper No 3

EDGERTON L., (1986) "Public Protest, Domestic Acquiescence: Women in Northern Ireland" in R. Ridd and H. Calloway (Eds), *Caught up in Conflict: Women's Responses to Political Strife*, London: Macmillan

EVASON E., (1980) *Just Me and the Kids: A Study of Single Parent Families in Northern Ireland*, Belfast: EOCNI

EVASON E., (1982) *Hidden Violence: Battered Women in Northern Ireland*, Belfast: Farset Co-operative Press

EVASON E., (1986) "Poverty in Northern Ireland", *Studies*, 75

EVASON E., (1987) "Women and Social Security in Ireland" in C. Curtin, P. Jackson and B. O'Connor (Eds), *Gender in Irish Society*, Galway: Galway University Press

GAFFIKIN F. and MORRISSEY M., (1990) *Northern Ireland: the Thatcher Years*, London: Zed Press

GLENDINNING J. and MILLAR J., (1987) (Eds) *Women in Poverty in the United Kingdom*, Brighton: Wheatsheaf

GLENNERSTER H., (1983) (Ed) *The Future of the Welfare State*, London: Heinemann

GRAHAM H., (1984) *Women, Health and the Family*, Brighton: Wheatsheaf

GREGORY J., (1987) *Sex, Race and the Law*, London: Sage

HANMER J. and MAYNARD M., (1987) (Eds) *Women, Violence and Social Control*, London: Macmillan

KELLY L., (1988) *Surviving Sexual Violence*, Cambridge: Polity Press

LACEY N., (1987) "Legislation against Sex Discrimination: Questions from a Feminist Perspective", *Journal of Law and Society*, 14 (4)

LISTER R., (1990) *Citizens All?*, Bradford: University of Bradford, Inaugural Lecture, 13 March

McSHANE E. and PINKERTON J., (1986) "The Family in Northern Ireland", *Studies*, Summer

MISHRA R., (1986) "The Left and the Welfare State: a Critical Analysis", *Critical Social Policy*, 15

MITCHISON A., (1988) "Ulster's Family Feminists", *New Society*, 19 February

OSBORNE R. and CORMACK R., (1989) "Fair Employment: towards Reform in Northern Ireland", *Policy and Politics*, 17 (4)

NORTHERN IRELAND CENSUS OF POPULATION, "Economic Activity Tables", Belfast, HMSO

PASCALL, G., (1986) *Social Policy: a Feminist's Analysis*, London: Tavistock

POLICY, PLANNING AND RESEARCH UNIT, (1989) *Northern Ireland Abstract of Statistics*, Belfast: PPRU

REES T., (1983) "Boys off the Street and Girls in the Home: Youth Unemployment and State Intervention in Northern Ireland", in R. Fiddy (Ed), *In Place of Work: Policy and Provision for the Young Unemployed*, Lewes: Falmer Press

REGIONAL TRENDS, (1989) London: CSO

RIDD R. and CALLOWAY H., (1986) (Eds) *Caught up in Conflict: Women's Responses to Political Strife*, London: Macmillan

TOWNSEND P., (1979) *Poverty in the United Kingdom*, Harmondsworth: Penguin

TOWNSEND P., (1984) *Why Are the Many Poor?*, London: Fabian Society Tract 500

TREWSDALE J., (1983) "The Role of Women in the Northern Ireland Economy", in R. J. Cormack and R. D. Osborne (Eds), *Religion, Education and Employment: Aspects of Inequality in Northern Ireland*, Belfast: Appletree Press

TREWSDALE J., (1988) *Womanpower No 4: The Aftermath of Recession*, Belfast: EOCNI

WALBY S., (1986) *Patriarchy at Work*, Cambridge: Polity Press

WALBY S., (1990) *Theorizing Patriarchy*, Oxford: Basil Blackwell

WALKER A., (1982) "The Meaning and Social Division of Community Care", in A. Walker (Ed), *Community Care: the Family, the State and Social Policy*, Oxford: Basil Blackwell

WALKER A., (1984) *Social Planning. A Strategy for Socialist Welfare*, Oxford: Basil Blackwell

WARD M., (1983) *Unmanageable Revolutionaries: Women and Irish Nationalism, Ireland*, Brandon

WILLIAMS F., (1989) *Social Policy: A Critical Introduction*, Cambridge: Polity Press

# CHAPTER TWO

# WOMEN'S PAID WORK AND THE SEXUAL DIVISION OF LABOUR*

## MONICA McWILLIAMS

## INTRODUCTION

To date, very little research in Northern Ireland has investigated changes which are occurring within and between families as a result of the decline in employment for men and the increase for women since the Second World War. In Great Britain, the Women and Employment Survey generated immensely important information about female participation in the labour force and the complexity of decision-making about employment for women (Martin and Roberts, 1984). This study was not extended to Northern Ireland and as a consequence much less is known about such complexity here. The purpose of this Chapter is to fill in some of the resultant gap by providing information on married or cohabiting working-age men and women in Northern Ireland. In particular, the focus is on the interaction between married men and married women's employment or unemployment. Some insights are provided on what the world of work looks like for women in Northern Ireland - in both the formal and the domestic economy and comparisons are made with women working in Great Britain. The nature and extent of family responsibilities, the type of work in which women are engaged and the level of demand for female labour are all considered. Other issues, however, remain on the agenda and are identified for further research.

Where research on employment has taken place in Northern Ireland, its tendency to date has been to focus either on religion or on gender (Teague, 1987; Trewsdale, 1988). This Chapter will attempt to address some of the imbalance by highlighting differences as well as similarities between Catholic and Protestant women. Similarly, where unemployment has been referred to in much of the literature, it is higher Catholic male unemployment on which attention has been focused (Department of Economic Development, (DED) 1987). What this Chapter shows, however, is that the unemployment of the male partner affects the employment prospects of his partner. Male unemployment then not only affects the husband, but often also the wife. One conclusion which will be drawn from this is that the emphasis within social and economic policy needs to change. The opportunity for work or training, or the decision about who should receive income support, is as relevant to married women as it is to married men. Since the sexual division of labour, like the "religious" division of labour, has far-reaching implications for patterns of employment, household income and family policy, the contention here is that more attention needs to be paid to it. The final Section then will recommend a number of policy changes in the light of the reported findings.

The focus of this Chapter is on married or cohabiting men and women below retirement age. Data are in the main derived from secondary analyses carried out on data sets from three major surveys which took place in Northern Ireland in 1985-86. These were the Continuous Household Survey (CHS), which included a sample of 1,554 couples; the Northern Ireland's Housing Executive's Household Surveys (NIHEHS) (both Regional and Belfast) with a total sample of 14,256 married couples; and the Labour Force Survey (LFS) covering 1,918 couples. The analysis will distinguish four household arrangements based on the nature of the division of (paid) labour. First, where both partners are working; second where neither partner is in waged work; third, where only the male partner is working; and finally where only the female partner is employed. For the sake of brevity it will be easier to refer to couples as dual earners; both unemployed; male breadwinner; and female breadwinner. Although we use these categories, it must be remembered that "work" is operationalised as paid employment only in these categories, and that for information on unpaid work in the household, other sources must be used.

## The Division of (Paid) Labour

The division of labour most common amongst households as reported in all three surveys is the dual earner couple. This is followed by the male breadwinner, with unemployed couples and the female breadwinner being less prevalent.

Table 2.1:  Households with an Economically Active Couple, 1985

|  | Continuous Household Survey % | Housing Executive Survey % | Labour Force Survey % |
|---|---|---|---|
| Dual Earners | 43 | 39 | 55 |
| Male Breadwinner | 40 | 38 | 33 |
| Both Unemployed | 14 | 18 | 9 |
| Female Breadwinner | 3 | 5 | 3 |
| Base (all couples) | 1,554 | 14,256 | 1,918 |

Note: The LFS considers one or more hours for which a person is in receipt of payment as paid work. The CHS and the NIHEHS apply a more rigorous interpretation of employment which explains much of the differential in economic activity between these surveys on the one hand and the LFS on the other.

Sources:  PPRU, CHS (NI) , 1985; NIHEHS, 1985; DED, LFS, 1985

The stereotypical view of families in Northern Ireland as "man in the labour market and woman in the home" is therefore receding, and to the extent that social policies continue to be predicated on the belief that the male breadwinner is the dominant family pattern, they are out of date and inappropriate.

Turning to patterns of male unemployment and female employment, Table 2.1 also suggests that the idea that male unemployment results in a pattern of female breadwinners must be challenged. Female breadwinner couples account for between three and five per cent only and the likelihood that both partners will be unemployed is much greater than the likelihood that the woman will be the breadwinner. Other Northern Ireland data serve to confirm this, challenging the popular images of female breadwinners in some areas of high male unemployment (McLaughlin 1987, 1989) and showing that where the husband is unemployed, the wife is likely to be unemployed also (McLaughlin, Millar and Cooke, 1989).

Table 2.2 shows that the level of unemployment for couples in Northern Ireland is high, considerably higher than that recorded by the General Household Survey (GHS) in Great Britain.

Table 2.2:   Comparison of Economically Active Couples in Great
Britain and Northern Ireland, 1985

|  | Northern Ireland % | Great Britain % |
|---|---|---|
| Dual Earners | 43 | 55 |
| Male Breadwinner | 40 | 31 |
| Both Unemployed | 14 | 10 |
| Female Breadwinner | 3 | 4 |
| All | 100 | 100 |
| Base (couples) | 1,554 | 4,813 |

Source:  PPRU, CHS (NI), 1985
OPCS, GHS, 1988

However, the proportion of female breadwinners seems to be about  the
same.  One might well ask why this is the case, when there are those who
assume that, with higher male unemployment together  with these "days
of equality", women will replace their partners  in the labour market. The
picture, however, is rather more complicated.

   In the first place, it is quite clear that in Northern Ireland, as in
Great Britain and indeed elsewhere, women do not replace men in the
labour market.  The separation between "men's jobs" and "women's
jobs", and the strong pattern of gender segregation in occupations is
demonstrated in more detail later in the Chapter.  In the second place, the
"women's jobs" that are available do not attract a "family wage".  They
are predominantly low-paid jobs, often part-time and with few or no prospects
for advancement.  There is further material on this both in this Chapter and
in Chapter Three by Hazel Morrissey.  Thirdly, there is the matter of
benefit disincentives.  As a wife's earnings rise above a certain (low)
level, so, pound for pound, her unemployed husband's benefits are reduced.  Fourthly, there is the question of family size.  If family size is
higher among those couples who are both unemployed, and later this is
shown to be the case (Table 2.5), and if childcare responsibilities inhibit
women from entering the market for paid labour (See Tables 2.5 and 2.6),
this too may be a factor enhancing the size of the "both  unemployed"
group and reducing the likelihood of female breadwinners.  We can note

in this connection that there is no evidence that unemployed men in Northern Ireland find an alternative role in housework or childcare, and in most cases both partners continue to adopt a traditional sexual division of labour in the face of male unemployment (McLaughlin, 1987, 1989; McLaughlin and Millar, 1987). The stability of the sexual division of labour in the home in the face of women's changing employment patterns is also found on a widespread basis in British studies (Morris, 1990).

There are still other factors to take into account here, such as age and religion. Differences between the two religious communities are discussed further in the next Section. A breakdown by age (not shown here), suggests that in the minority of cases where the wife does become the breadwinner, she is likely to be older (45-65 years) and hence, of course, less likely to have dependent children.

In all, factors such as the nature and level of demand for women's labour, the potential earning power of women, the operation of the benefits system and male unemployment, the number and ages of children and the level of childcare, are all likely to affect the patterns of paid employment among couples. Historical, cultural and ideological factors also enter this complex fabric particularly when one considers the influence of Church and State in the Northern Ireland context (See below). We now turn to consider, as far as the material from the three surveys will allow, how these matters impinge more specifically on the labour market participation of women themselves.

## Women in the Labour Market

The consistently higher levels of unemployment in Northern Ireland than in Great Britain, and the decline in manufacturing  industry, encouraged the Northern Ireland Government in the 1960s and early 1970s to pursue a development strategy which would attract investment for male employment. Not only did female workers lose their jobs in the clothing and textile industries in the post-war period (jobs which had kept women's employment relatively high in the first part of the century), they also failed to benefit to the same extent as British women from the experience of war-time employment. Jane Lewis (1984) shows that  what emerged from this experience in Great Britain was the possibility for women to combine work, marriage and motherhood. In Northern Ireland, a more conservative ideology operating within government in conjunction with the major churches reiterated the prime role of women as mothers and homemakers (de Frinze, 1985; O'Dowd, 1987). The expectation that married women would give up paid employment was enforced through marriage bars which prevented women from working in certain occupations. In the civil service, for example, these were not abolished until the early 1970s.

Consequently, in 1971, as Census data show, only 29 per cent of married women were economically active in Northern Ireland compared to 42 per cent in Great Britain (Compton, 1986). The differential in the economic activity rate of married women in Northern Ireland is now much less pronounced, and is mainly due to a shift in government policy in the 1970s which resulted in an expansion of public services in Northern Ireland. A particular feature of this expansion is that Catholics and women of both religions increased their numbers in employment, though it remains the case today that both are seriously underrepresented at the more senior levels (Osborne, 1990).

During the 1980s in Northern Ireland when the demand for male employment was declining, married women were entering the labour market in larger numbers than ever before. What is clear is that they were not taking up "men's jobs" as some traditionalists were still arguing. Rather they were entering jobs that were rarely considered by men because of their low pay, temporary, part-time and "female-typed" status. Moreover, data from the three surveys on part-time and full-time work show that men are employed full-time, while their female partners are nearly equally likely to be in full- or part-time employment. Table 2.3 sets out the position as shown in the CHS.

Table 2.3: Economic Activity of Partners, 1985

|  | Males | | Females | |
| --- | --- | --- | --- | --- |
|  | % | N | % | N |
| Working full-time | 80 | 1,249 | 26 | 404 |
| Working part-time | 2 | 34 | 20 | 318 |
| Unemployed | 17 | 261 | 4 | 56 |
| Keeping house | 1 | 10 | 50 | 776 |
| Total | 100 | 1,554 | 100 | 1,554 |

Source:  PPRU, CHS (NI), 1985

Although there has been an increase in the participation of women in the labour market throughout the 1970s and 1980s, it is also worth noting, as Table 2.3 shows, that half of all married women still record themselves as keeping house, or retired, even though they are under 60 years of age. Osborne and Cormack (1989) have shown that even a sizeable proportion (13 per cent) of young women (between 16-24) record that they are keeping house compared to no young men who place themselves in this category. Further research is needed to ascertain whether women in Northern Ireland find an alternative and preferred definition to unemployment in the status of "keeping house" or whether they are actually more actively engaged (or see themselves as so) in domestic/caring activities than other (employed and unemployed) women.

It would appear (Table 2.4) that women in Northern Ireland tend to be slightly more "traditional" in their labour market behaviour than women in Great Britain, insofar as the proportions classed as economically inactive are considerably higher. On the other hand, Table 2.4 also shows quite clearly that it is in relation to part-time work only that the difference between Northern Ireland and Great Britain occurs. Whether these patterns reflect differences in attitudes, family responsibilities or job opportunities is debatable. In relation to the last of these, an enduring weakness of the Northern Ireland economy has been its inability to generate employment opportunities on a par with the growth of the local labour force. As the manufacturing sector has continued to decline, opportunities for migration have diminished, and as surplus workers continued to be created, then "unemployment" may take a disguised form due to a fall in activity rates, particularly for females. Perceptions amongst some women that there are no jobs available are likely to affect the number of married women seeking employment and registering as unemployed, as indeed have the recent changes in eligibility for social security benefits. It may be this assessment that leads them ultimately to be classed as "economically inactive" rather than a traditional adherence to the role of housewife and mother which to date has been the more widely accepted explanation for this large group of women. Whether women in the categories "economically inactive" or "keeping house" may actually be available for work in certain circumstances remains an open question.

Table 2.4:   The Economic Activity of Married Couples, 1985

|  | All Husbands | | Husbands Working | |
|  | GB | NI | GB | NI |
|  | % | % | % | % |
|---|---|---|---|---|
| Wife working: | | | | |
| Full-time | 27 | 26 | 28 | 29 |
| Part-time | 32 | 20 | 34 | 23 |
| Wife unemployed | 4 | 4 | 3 | 3 |
| Wife economically inactive | 37 | 50 | 34 | 45 |
| Base (couples) | 4,319 | 1,283 | | |

Sources:   PPRU, CHS (NI), 1985
OPCS, GHS, 1988

There are also important differences between the Protestant and Catholic communities as far as women's paid employment is concerned. The percentage of unemployed couples is higher amongst Catholics whilst dual earners are more likely amongst Protestants, particularly where the second earner works part-time. Published tables from the CHS show that among economically active women, a rather smaller proportion of Catholic women (30 per cent) work part-time compared with 34 per cent of Protestant women (CHS, 1989a). One explanation for this is the disincentive for wives of unemployed men (disproportionately Catholic) to take up or retain part-time employment since their husband's benefit would be reduced. Not only then is the interaction of unemployment between husbands and wives important but so too is its concentration amongst particular families. Unemployment affects more Catholic families than Protestants and in turn leaves both the men and women in these families worse off. Moreover, the proportion of Catholic families in receipt of supplementary benefit rose significantly from 1983 to 1987 (from 32 per cent to 37 per cent), whilst the proportion of Protestant families in this situation (increasing from 19 per cent to 20 per cent) remained virtually the same (CHS, 1989a). Although it would be mistaken to account for higher levels of female Catholic non-employment by reference to male Catholic unemployment alone, what this does show is that the interaction of gender and religion are important determinants in the increasing inequalities which are occurring between households in Northern Ireland. Overall, it is the lower economic activity rate of married Catholic women that depresses the average for Northern Ireland compared with Great Britain, since Protestant women have similar levels of activity to women in Great Britain (60 per cent of Protestant women aged 25 to 44 are economically active compared with 42 per cent of Catholic women of the same age, DED, 1986). Ideally, exploration is needed of the extent to which differences between Northern Ireland and Great Britain, and within Northern Ireland, differences between Catholic and Protestant women, can be accounted for by different attitudes to employment, different levels of family responsibilities or, of course, by differences in job opportunities in each case. In practice, the three surveys drawn upon here allowed some consideration of the role of family responsibilities and of job opportunities, and these are considered in turn.

### Family Responsibilities

A number of studies in Great Britain have demonstrated that a major structural factor underlying women's participation in employment is their continued responsibility for childcare. Lonsdale (1985) shows that the arrival of children is a very serious impediment to the employment prospects of females; Joshi (1987) has examined the effects of family formation on women's lifetime earnings through secondary analysis of the Women and Employment Survey. Joshi shows that having children in Great Britain can cost a woman up to half her lifetime's potential earnings, while men's employment experience and earnings are largely unaffected by fatherhood and may even be enhanced by marriage. Unfortunately we do not have similar work-history data for women (and their partners) in Northern Ireland. Neither do we have detailed information on the spacing of children or the length of time a woman is out of employment when she has children. And hence we cannot calculate the cost of parenthood for women in Northern Ireland.

What information we do have gives us rough indications of the degree of importance of family size in relation to women's employment. Catholic women's lower economic activity rate (See earlier) compared with Protestant women should be placed in the context of their higher fertility rates as well as their higher likelihood of marriage to an unemployed man. The Northern Ireland Fertility Study indicated that disparities in family size are a function of different attitudes operating between Catholics and Protestants on the question of fertility. However, it is also true that there has been substantial convergence of family size between Catholics and Protestants since the 1970s (Compton and Coward, 1989).

Employment of married women, upward social mobility and improvements in educational attainment have all in general been shown to exert a downward pressure on family sizes and birth rates (Ermisch, 1983). In Northern Ireland, family size has not increased, and one might expect some convergence to take place in the fertility rate of women in Northern Ireland and Great Britain which, other things being equal, in turn might be reflected in the narrowing of economic activity rates. The point needs to be stressed, however, that any decrease in fertility rates may not necessarily lead to an increase in economic activity, since it may not only be the number of children *per se* which constitutes the obstacle to employment but also difficulties in arranging childcare whether for one, two or three children, together with differential access to job opportunities for women in Northern Ireland compared with Great Britain.

The Northern Ireland data confirm findings by Martin and Roberts (1984) for Great Britain, that there is evidence of a definite association between the employment status of a couple and the number of dependents in the home. As might be expected in Northern Ireland, too, those households in which both partners are in paid employment have the lowest number of children under 16. As Table 2.5 shows, nearly two-thirds of dual earner and female breadwinner couples have none or only one dependent child whereas this is the case in only 47 and 35 per cent of male breadwinner and unemployed couples respectively.

Table 2.5:  Couples' Employment Status by Number of
Children under 16

| Number of Children Under 16 | All Couples | Dual Earners | Both Unemployed | Male Bread-winner | Female Bread-winner |
|---|---|---|---|---|---|
| | % | % | % | % | % |
| None | 32 | 41 | 15 | 28 | 31 |
| One | 21 | 23 | 20 | 19 | 29 |
| Two | 23 | 20 | 28 | 25 | 16 |
| Three or more | 24 | 16 | 36 | 28 | 24 |
| Base | 1,554 | 613 | 222 | 610 | 49 |

Source:  PPRU, CHS (NI), 1985

Despite this impact of the number of children in reducing women's employment participation, it is the age of the youngest child which is a major determinant of women's employment status. Table 2.6 confirms this but also shows an interesting and important difference between Great Britain and Northern Ireland. Women with a youngest child aged 0 to 4 have similarly low employment activity rates (28 per cent) in both Northern Ireland and Great Britain. But women with a youngest child of school age are less likely to be in employment in Northern Ireland than in Great Britain. Activity rates in the two countries then begin to converge again after the youngest child reaches 16.

Table 2.6:   Employment Activity Rate of Females with Dependent Children by Age of Youngest Child

| Age of Youngest Child | Northern Ireland | Great Britain | % Difference with Great Britain |
|---|---|---|---|
| 0 - 4 | 28 | 28 | |
| 5 - 10 | 45 | 58 | -13 |
| 11 - 15 | 55 | 69 | -14 |
| 16 - 18 | 64 | 70 | - 6 |
| All with children | 40 | 50 | -10 |

Note: The Employment Activity Rate is based on the proportion of those actually in work as opposed to the Economic Activity Rate based on those in work and those seeking work.

Source:  LFS Northern Ireland and Great Britain, 1985, Adapted from Cohen (1988)

This difference may well be a reflection of both the lower availability of part-time work for women in Northern Ireland than in Great Britain and also the negative impact of male unemployment on wives' take-up of part-time work (See earlier). It is also, however, likely to be a reflection of the availability (or rather, in the case of Northern Ireland, the lack of availability) of childcare. In her Chapter in this volume, Bronagh Hinds has shown Northern Ireland's poor record on childcare provision and documents a set of assumptions underpinning policy in this area which are far from regarding provision as a positive factor in facilitating women's paid employment.

Responsibilities for children should not, however, be attributed a solely deterministic role in relation to women's employment in Northern Ireland. Interestingly, despite Northern Ireland's larger family size, proportionately more women who are economically active work full-time in Northern Ireland than in Great Britain. Given the types of jobs on offer, combined with the cost of childcare, however, many women must still engage in a mental accounting procedure of whether it is worthwhile working. Brannen and Moss (1987) have shown that the cost of childcare and the cost of the dual earner lifestyle are not described by women in Great Britain as necessary household expenditure but as the ''price'' women must pay for working.

It is also the case that the absence of good quality appropriate and reasonable childcare and the weight of the double burden on women adversely affects the quality of their participation through locking them into low paid, less responsible, more restrictive jobs (See Chapter Three). A study in the Northern Ireland Civil Service (NICS) shows that 25 per cent of women who were eligible for promotion chose not to go forward. They were reported as particularly likely to opt out where the promotion involved a change of location, or an increase in the difficulties of combining work and home responsibilities (NICS, 1990). The division of labour within the home, particularly where there are small children, can directly affect the division of labour in the more formal economy. The effect of trying to combine poor childcare together with poor access to training (See McCorry, 1988, and for young women, Chapter Seven by Pamela Montgomery) does mean that for many women their employment options are restricted. These are the women who often have to choose low status and/or part-time jobs. It is also the case, as the next Section shows, that increasingly these are the only jobs on offer.

## Job Opportunities for Women

In Northern Ireland, as in Great Britain, the increase in women's employment has been mainly the result of a part-time job explosion over the last 20 years, as Table 2.7 shows. Nevertheless the proportion of all female jobs which are part-time in Northern Ireland (37 per cent) is still considerably smaller than in Great Britain (42 per cent).

Table 2.7:   Female Employees in Employment in Great Britain
and Northern Ireland:   Changes between 1981-87

| | Great Britain (000's) | | | |
|---|---|---|---|---|
| | 1981 | 1984 | 1987 | % change 1981-87 |
| Full-time jobs | 5,304 | 4,956 | 5,592 | + 5 |
| Part-time jobs | 3,781 | 4,282 | 4,121 | + 9 |
| Total jobs | 9,085 | 9,238 | 9,713 | + 7 |
| Part time jobs as a % of all jobs | 42 | 46 | 42 | |
| | Northern Ireland (000's) | | | |
| | 1981 | 1984 | 1987 | % change 1981-87 |
| Full-time jobs | 147 | 147 | 149 | + 2 |
| Part-time jobs | 78 | 81 | 90 | +15 |
| Total jobs | 225 | 228 | 239 | + 6 |
| Part time jobs as a % of all jobs | 35 | 36 | 37 | |

Sources:   Censuses of Employment (various), DED Statistics  Notices (1989) and Employment Gazette, November 1989

As we have noted previously, what this means is that despite the larger family size in Northern Ireland, proportionately more  married women who are working are working full-time than part-time thus reflecting the demand for labour.  Moreover, the importance of labour demand in influencing women's supply may be particularly important to women with employed husbands.  It is these women who are more likely to be available for both full-time and part-time work, thus increasing the family income through a secondary wage.  Although these structural changes in the labour market are benefiting women, it is worth emphasising that they are benefiting some women more than others (women with employed partners rather than women with unemployed partners) and that even amongst these women, divisions are being created between those in career structures as compared to low wage earners (See Chapter Three).

Increasingly, a two-tier system of women's employment is operating throughout Northern Ireland. This duality in the female labour market has been described as an "upstairs" and "downstairs" division between women workers (McCormack, 1989). The divergent status and earning power of women within the service sector, for example, is reflected in the fact that female manual workers in Northern Ireland are the lowest paid in the United Kingdom, whilst non-manual women, mainly in banking, finance and insurance, are amongst the highest paid (See Chapter Three).

Even within this small minority of higher female earners, it is most unlikely that wives earn as much as their husbands. It was not possible directly to analyse women's incomes from the data in the three surveys, but the information available lent little support to the suggestion that there is an increasing tendency for husbands and wives to have occupations of a similar status. The pattern emerging is more indicative, therefore, of the continued subordination of the majority of women in this regard.

A further depressing feature is that despite increases in service sector employment, more women have also become unemployed in the 1980s. This is partially due to the increase in unemployment amongst their partners which in turn may lead to their own unemployment. However, it can also be attributed to job loss in semi-skilled operative jobs and to recent cuts in public sector employment. In 1985, 50 per cent of all female employees worked in social services, in health and education, in the civil service and local government. Catholic workers and women in particular benefited from the expansion of these jobs. By 1989, however, public expenditure cutbacks were taking effect in Northern Ireland, causing an overall job decline of four per cent in the health and social services. In practice this has meant that, over the four-year period, 2,746 women have lost their jobs in this sector (DED, 1990). Many of these jobs were in the administration of social security which has been increasingly computerised but some job loss has also been consequent on the privatisation of the health service. Due to the growth in service sector jobs, it is often thought that unemployment is not an issue for women. This, however, is clearly not the case. Moreover, those women who began to gain entry to the public sector are now the same women who are being made redundant. These women are in the main, ancillary workers and more likely to be Catholic than Protestant. At a time when the government in Northern Ireland is promoting investment for Catholic employment to compensate for the lack of employment in mainly Catholic areas, public sector employment is being cut and is directly impinging on the lives of those for whom government explicitly states it is concerned.

For the future, segregation in the labour market is likely to continue, particularly if part-time employment increases. Twenty-three per cent of all employees at present are part-time - the majority of whom are female (75 per cent) (DED, 1989). Interestingly, the proportion of all jobs which are part-time is the same as in Great Britain, but the proportion of males in part-time work is different. In Great Britain, 17 per cent of all part-time jobs are carried out by men; this compares with 25 per cent in Northern Ireland. We can only speculate as to whether or not higher rates of unemployment in Northern Ireland are encouraging more men to familiarise themselves with the world of part-time work, as Norman Fowler, the then Minister for Health and Social Security, recommended in his Green Paper (HMSO, 1985). In doing so, they may be using part-time work as a stepping stone to secure more permanent employment. We cannot know if they are displacing women from part-time jobs since this type of work has traditionally been associated with females. It could be argued that since one in ten men is now employed part-time in Northern Ireland, a different "job plan" is becoming evident among men as well as women. It may be pure speculation to envisage a future where both sexes adopt complex cycles of work - moving from full-time to part-time and vice versa.

One thing which is certain is that part-time work will increasingly be employer-led, with women - and presumably men - having even less choice about the number and pattern of hours which they work. As employers strive towards greater flexibility, many part-time workers will be likely to be held just below the threshold of hours required for employment and social security protection. As women continue to fit in, and be fitted in, with employment that revolves around their families' needs, they could find their access to pensions, maternity leave and sick pay further restricted. A distinction will be maintained between those employees who are able to secure some investment for the future and those who are not. Increasingly, divisions will be created between women themselves, not just as wage earners but as pensioners. The proposed European Directive on *pro rata* rights with full-time workers would help to guarantee the occupational welfare of part-timers. It could also encourage more women to become full-time employees, since any posts which became vacant would be offered to them. It is significant that Great Britain continues to veto this Directive when part-time employment is a particularly British (and Northern Irish) phenomenon (Dex & Shaw, 1988). Part-time work is a solution for those women (and less often men) who want to reconcile the many demands involved in being a parent and an employee but it is also an economic solution for employers, and it is in this dual function that its contradictory character for women lies.

## Concluding Remarks

The labour market in Northern Ireland is in a process of greater change now than at any time in the previous 40 years.  Within  Great Britain and in Northern Ireland women have increased as a  proportion of the civilian labour force - though the increase  has been somewhat greater during the 1980s for women in Great Britain.  This situation is likely to change in the future; between 1988-2000, it is estimated that the proportion of women in the labour force will increase by a further 13 per cent in Northern Ireland compared with eight per cent in Great Britain.  By the turn of the next century, then, 300,000 women will be in work or available for work in Northern Ireland and they will constitute 40 per cent of the labour force. If the self-employed and unemployed are excluded from this, female employees will make-up nearly half of all those in work (Employment Gazette, 1990).

Despite these past and predicted future increases, desegregated workplaces and convergence of skills between men and women have not so far materialised.  If anything, the skills content of female manual jobs has declined.  The increase in part-time employment and deregulation of the labour market are creating a situation where the greater availability of work for women does not necessarily ensure a higher income or better conditions of service.

Current social security regulations which deduct part of a wife's earned income from an unemployed husband's benefit act as a considerable economic disincentive in this situation for women to search for waged employment.  Social security provision during male unemployment also discourages wives from staying in paid work - resulting in more unemployed couples than would otherwise  be the case. This is a very negative policy in terms of women's own position and that of the family as a whole. The present promotion of family credit which is targetted at unemployed family men does the opposite of what is needed since it is based on the presumption of male breadwinners.  There are major problems with this benefit mainly in relation to low take-up and eligibility rules and, on top of this, family credit will never raise family income to comparable levels to that of dual earner couples.

What we need are policies which treat women's employment seriously.  First, such policies must increase women's financial  independence and personal incomes. If there is no evidence to support the comforting idea that households share their labour and resources equally, then social policy must compensate accordingly to increase the standard of living of all in Northern Ireland (cf. Evason, Chapter Four). Secondly, until more data become available, we can only speculate on the extent to which working wives keep families out of poverty. In Northern Ireland, households dependent on social security or lacking a secondary worker are not only likely to be experiencing poverty but also to be relatively worse off than other households in the United Kingdom. At the other end of the scale, the higher incomes enjoyed by dual earner households contribute substantially to a higher standard of living amongst these families. What we have shown here is that the separation of families into "dual worker" and "no worker" types is a major source of division in Northern Ireland. Divisions then are being accentuated between families and moreover between Catholic and Protestant families. The present concern about the "no earner" male within these families, however, needs to be extended to include the "no earner" female. As we have shown earlier, higher male unemployment amongst Catholics in turn means that more Catholic married women are unemployed and indeed, they remain so for longer periods of time than their Protestant counterparts (CHS, 1989). What needs to be emphasised is that we should be developing policies which lessen the economic and social divide between Catholic and Protestant women and not just between Catholic and Protestant men.

Employment policies which might address this situation would involve higher, not lower, public expenditure alongside the existing emphasis on attracting private investment. For both men and women, specific action is needed to counteract the "no earner" phenomenon. Both partners should be offered interviews for employment, without treating the unemployed man as somehow separate from the couple (McLaughlin et al, 1989). Attention should also be focused on the non-employment, and less often, registered unemployment, of wives by all employment development agencies (McLaughlin, 1989). Rather than search for ways of discounting married women from official statistics, it is important to regard them as an integral part of the family's labour resources, particularly where unemployment is concerned. This would reap quantifiable benefits for employers by preventing the disappearance of women's education, training, experience and potential from the labour market.

Finally, we need support structures both at home and at work. As long as conflict continues over who does what in the home, women will neither have the confidence nor the energy to take on more work (Hochschild,

1989). Male unemployment does not seem, in itself, to create the conditions for a more equal sharing of domestic responsibilities. Alongside material and structural changes, a shift in ideology must also take place. Change is necessary in the attitudes and practice of men towards the work involved in rearing their own families if the existing division of labour is not to be reproduced in the next generation. Job packages which involve less overtime, a shorter working week, paternity and parental leave provide the conditions under which fathers can in principle share in the care of their children. We also need a stronger childcare policy to allow women to get and to hold onto better jobs than they have at present. Not only is this important in terms of reducing occupational gender inequality *per se*, but the reduction of that inequality would mean in the long-term, that women are better equipped to become sole breadwinners in the event of male unemployment and disability or marital break-up. This in turn would reduce the burden on social security. Some countries can now offer us models of good practice where education, employment legislation and social security all combine to break down the barriers between home and labour market. Not only do these facilitate greater equality of opportunity but they exemplify a more efficient usage of human resources. What we need now is to develop a coherent set of social policies which will enable men and women in Northern Ireland to participate in all forms of work and for the work itself to be more equitably distributed.

**\*  Acknowledgement**

The material from which this Chapter is drawn was gathered as part of a project funded by the Equal Opportunities Commission for Northern Ireland entitled *"Women and the World of Work in Northern Ireland"* and carried out by this author, together with Rona Campbell and Mike Morrissey. The help of the EOCNI and of the providers of statistical tables from the three surveys is gratefully acknowledged.

# REFERENCES

BRANNEN J. and MOSS P., (1987) "Dual Earner Households" in Brannen J. and Wilson G., (Eds) *Give and Take in Families*, London: Allen and Unwin

COHEN B., (1988) *Caring for Children: Services and Policies for Childcare and Equal Opportunities in the United Kingdom*, London: Commission of the European Communities

COMPTON P., (1986) *Demographic Trends in Northern Ireland*, Report 57, Belfast: NIEC

COMPTON P. and COWARD J., (1989) *Fertility and Family Planning in Northern Ireland*, Aldershot: Avebury

DEPARTMENT OF ECONOMIC DEVELOPMENT, (1985) *Labour Force Survey*, Unpublished table, Belfast: HMSO

DEPARTMENT OF ECONOMIC DEVELOPMENT, (1987) *Consultative Document on Equality of Opportunity*, Belfast: HMSO

DEPARTMENT OF ECONOMIC DEVELOPMENT, (various dates) "Census of Employment. Statistics Notices", Belfast, Netherleigh: Statistics Branch

DEPARTMENT OF ECONOMIC DEVELOPMENT, (1990) "Employees in Employment, December 1989. Statistics Notice", Belfast, Netherleigh: Statistics Branch

De FRINZE M., (1986) "Sex Differentials in the Northern Ireland Economy 1963-78", unpublished MA thesis, University of Ulster at Jordanstown

DEX S. and SHAW L. B., (1988) "Women's Working Lives: A Comparison of Women in the USA and Britain", in Hunt A., (Ed) *Women and Paid Work: Issues in Equality*, London: Macmillan

EMPLOYMENT GAZETTE, (1989) "1989 Census of Employment Results for Great Britain", November

EMPLOYMENT GAZETTE, (1990) "Regional Labour Force Outlook to the Year 2000", January

ERMISCH J., (1983) *The Political Economy of Demographic Change*, London: Heinemann

GREEN PAPER, (1985) *Reform of Social Security*, Vol 1, Cmnd 9517, London: HMSO

HOCHSCHILD A., (1989) *The Second Shift: Working Parents and the Revolution at Home*, London: Penguin

JOSHI H., (1987) "The Cost of Caring" in Glendinning C. and Millar J., (Eds) *Women and Poverty in Britain*, Brighton: Wheatsheaf

LEWIS J., (1984) *Women in England 1870-1950*, Brighton: Wheatsheaf

LONSDALE J., (1985) *Work and Inequality*, London: Longman

McCORMACK I., (1989) "Irish Congress of Trade Unions Conference Report" (Motion by NUPE), Belfast: NUPE

McCORRY M., (1988) *Women and the Need for Training*, Belfast: Women's Education Project

McLAUGHLIN E., (1987) "Maiden City Blues", unpublished PhD thesis, Belfast: Queen's University of Belfast

McLAUGHLIN E., (1989) "In Search of the Female Breadwinner: Gender and Unemployment in Derry City", in Donnan H. and McFarlane G., (Eds) *Social Anthropology and Public Policy in Northern Ireland*, Aldershot: Avebury

McLAUGHLIN E. and MILLAR J., (1987) *The Determinants of Labour Supply in Long-Term Unemployment*, Belfast: Policy Research Institute

McLAUGHLIN E., MILLAR J. and COOKE K., (1989) *Work and Welfare Benefits*, Aldershot: Gower

MARTIN J. and ROBERTS C., (1984) *Women and Employment Survey*, London: HMSO

MORRIS L., (1990) *The Workings of the Household*, Cambridge: Polity Press

NORTHERN IRELAND CIVIL SERVICE, (1990) "Shrinking Violets? A Study of Non-Participation in Competition for Promotion in the Northern Ireland Civil Service", quoted in NIPSA News, March, Belfast: Harkin House

NORTHERN IRELAND HOUSING EXECUTIVE, (1985) "Household Survey", Unpublished table, Belfast: NIHE

O'DOWD L., (1987) "Church, State and Women", in Curtin C. et al, (Eds) *Gender in Irish Society*, Galway: Galway University Press

OFFICE OF POPULATION CENSUSES AND SURVEYS, (1988) *General Household Survey, 1985*, London: HMSO

OSBORNE R. D., (1990) "Equal Opportunities in the Northern Ireland Civil Service", *Public Money and Management*, 10, 2, pp 41-45

OSBORNE R. D. and CORMACK R. J., (1989) "Gender and Religion as Issues in Education, Training and Entry to Work", in Harbinson J., (Ed) *Growing Up in Northern Ireland*, Belfast: Stranmillis College

POLICY PLANNING AND RESEARCH UNIT, (1985) "Continuous Household Survey", Unpublished table, Belfast: Department of Finance and Personnel

POLICY PLANNING AND RESEARCH UNIT, (1989a) "Continuous Household Survey, Monitor No 1 on Religion", Belfast: Department of Finance and Personnel

POLICY PLANNING AND RESEARCH UNIT, (1989b) "Continuous Household Survey, Monitor No 3 Preliminary Results for 1988", Belfast: Department of Finance and Personnel

TEAGUE P., (1987), (Ed), *Beyond the Rhetoric: Politics, the Economy and Social Policy in Northern Ireland*, London: Lawrence and Wishart

TREWSDALE J., (1988) *Womanpower No 4: The Aftermath of the Recession*, Belfast: EOCNI

# CHAPTER THREE

# DIFFERENT SHARES: WOMEN, EMPLOYMENT AND EARNINGS

## HAZEL MORRISSEY

## INTRODUCTION

The purpose of this Chapter is to examine women's earnings and employment in Northern Ireland in the context of industrial and occupational change. The relationship between earnings and industrial structure in Northern Ireland is particularly interesting since Northern Ireland has traditionally been the lowest paying region in the United Kingdom, while it has simultaneously undergone considerable economic upheaval. The relatively low level of earnings can be attributed primarily to higher regional unemployment. Where the supply of labour continually outstrips the demand, its price will be lowered (Adnett, 1989). A further relevant factor is the predominance of unskilled manual work and the lack of educational qualifications of the workforce. Moreover, there is the widely held belief among management that profitability depends on holding down labour costs. Boosting productivity through investment in training and new technology has been a secondary consideration.

### Low Pay

There has been an ongoing debate on low pay (Craig et al, 1982) since the 1970s when it was discovered that many of the poor were in low paid work rather than dependent on state benefits (Evason, 1978). Calls for statutory regulation of wages, however, were rejected for different reasons by both Trade Unions and employers, and by Labour and Conservative Governments. Trade unions and the Labour Party argued that the lowest paying industries were those dominated by Wages Councils, which despite setting statutory minimum rates had failed to end low pay (Craig et al,

1982).  They preferred to rely on greater trade union organisation linked
to aggressive collective bargaining.  Latterly this position has changed
with the deregulation of the labour market and the reduction of trade union
power.  In the late 1980s and early 1990s the Labour Party and the TUC
have supported regulation of earnings and the introduction of a statutory
minimum wage through the operation of the European Social Charter.
Conservative Governments, since 1979, have linked pay levels to unemployment, arguing that by insisting on wage rises above the rate of inflation workers are pricing themselves out of employment (Novak, 1988).
Similarly, they have opposed any statutory regulation of earnings, consistently seeking to abolish the Wages Councils in response to lobbying from
the Institute of Directors and the Federation of Self Employed and Small
Businesses.

As part of the deregulation of the labour market in the 1980s, there
have been moves to end centralised pay bargaining and introduce regional
wage rates.  In practice, this has resulted in the earnings distribution
growing wider.  Skills shortages in certain industries and in the South East
of England have led to increases in real terms for skilled workers, while
the earnings of unskilled manual workers, particularly though not exclusively those in peripheral regions, have fallen further behind.

The position of female earnings appears to be following a similar
trend.  While it is true that the top ten percent of women in Great Britain
are earning over £15,000 a year (DED, 1989), the gap between male and
female earnings persists.  The gender differential in Great Britain is now
wider than at any time since the introduction of the Equal Pay Act in 1975
(EOC, 1989).  In 1988, average pay for women in Northern Ireland was
£141 a week - £70 less than the average male wage, and 32 per cent below
pay levels for women in the South East of England.  In 1989, non-manual
females earned only 63 per cent of the average hourly pay of their male
counterparts, while manual females earned 71 per cent of the average
hourly pay of male manual workers.

There are various ways of defining low pay.  Government has its
definition - Income Support (formerly Supplementary Benefit) earnings
equivalent.  The trade unions and poverty lobbies take two-thirds of median
male manual earnings as the benchmark (Low Pay Unit, 1988).  However,
the low pay definition which is gaining most acceptance is the Council of
Europe's "Decency Threshold".  This is based on the European Social
Charter which recognises the right of workers to a decent standard of
living.  A committee appointed by the Council works out a pay level for
each member state based on 68 per cent of national average adult earnings.

In 1989, average earnings in Northern Ireland were £206.65 (NES, 1989); accordingly the EC Decency Threshold would be £140.52 a week. In 1989, 50 per cent of all women full-time workers earned below £143 per week. In contrast, 25 per cent of men earned below £150 per week. On this basis, low pay in Northern Ireland is very much a female problem; and this would be even more so the case if part-time workers were included in the picture.

**Changing Industrial and Occupational Structures**

Gender differentials in pay are not uniform throughout the United Kingdom; they are overlaid by regional and sectoral divisions which must also be taken into account. These divisions are a result of a rapidly changing industrial structure, the recomposition of the workforce and the way work is organised. The conditions which gave rise to full employment prior to the 1970s will not recur in the same form. The days when entire economies could be dependent on heavy industry with vast workforces in individual factories are gone forever. Either the technology of the industry has changed, or the goods are produced in countries where labour costs are cheaper, and plants more modern and efficient than in the old industrial heartlands of Europe (European Commission, 1989).

Over recent decades Northern Ireland as a regional economy of the United Kingdom has experienced sharp industrial restructuring. This has entailed a further decline of its traditional manufacturing base and a growth of the service industries to a point where the public sector is now the main provider of jobs. Arguably the region is transforming from an industrial to a post-industrial society (Touraine, 1974; Blackaby, 1982; Gorz, 1982) with certain distinctive features and characteristics. Production contributes a declining share of Gross Domestic Product (GDP) while services become dominant. The decline of production has been common to a number of advanced industrial societies (Armstrong et al, 1984) but in Northern Ireland the process has been acute (Freeman, Gaffikin and Morrissey, 1988). Not only do services account for the bulk of GDP, they now account for around two-thirds of total employment in a sector which is increasingly dominated by female labour. This importance of female labour is not unusual for Northern Ireland, as females have played a significant role historically in the regional economy. The popular belief that the working-class in Northern Ireland was typified by the male engineering worker is simply untrue. The industrial revolution and factory production in Ireland was built primarily on linen and the labour of female textile workers before the engineering and shipbuilding industries emerged.  During the inter-war period there were two female linen workers for every male employed in shipbuilding and engineering (Morrissey, 1984).  In addition, with the outbreak of war in 1939, women became involved in types of employment formerly considered to be the preserve of men.  From riveting in the shipyard to train driving, women's employment extended far beyond their traditional occupations, and their earning power increased as a result.

However, in the post-war period, opportunities for paid employment began to retract as men returned to civilian life to reclaim their traditional jobs; war-time nursery provision ended, and the linen industry went into steep decline.  In the 1950s and 1960s efforts were made to get to grips with diversifying Northern Ireland's industrial base by attracting external capital.  This modernisation was geared to attracting replacement industries through generous grants and on the basis of a reputation for sound industrial relations.  Success was achieved in the establishment of new artificial fibre, telecommunications, rubber and chemical industries.  However, these replacement industries were differently located geographically and, in the main, employed men rather than women.  The large linen factories had been situated mainly in North and West Belfast, predominantly employing women, whereas the replacement industry of artificial fibres located new factories on the North East coast of Antrim and Derry and in North Armagh and employed a majority of men as process workers.

The political changes of the 1970s involved improving public services in an effort to create greater employment equality between the two communities and to establish parity with British services.  It is these two factors which help explain the growth and importance of the public sector in Northern Ireland.  Today it accounts for 40 per cent of all employees in employment.  Thus, it is a stabilising influence on the local economy and its importance in that respect can hardly be over-estimated.  The most recent plans for public spending show estimates of around £6 billion for 1990-91 (HM Treasury, 1990).  Without such expenditure the local economy would not only decline but would fall into Southern European levels of poverty and social provision.

The public sector has provided major opportunities for women to take paid employment.  In the 1970s, women who had formerly worked in manufacturing found it possible to get work as dinner ladies, canteen assistants, cleaners, and nursing auxiliaries.  Similarly, women who had been through third level education found employment as teachers, social workers, administrators, and health professionals.

The number of female employees has increased by 8.4 per cent over the last decade (Northern Ireland Abstract of Statistics 1984, 1989), they now make up 48 per cent of all employees in employment and account for 56.7 per cent in the public sector (DED, 1990). Table 3.1 shows how, in a period of recession, when unemployment reached 21 per cent of the insured population (January, 1986), women were still able to increase their overall employment by over 10,000. Employment declined in all sectors except for services where male employment grew by three per cent and female employment by five per cent.

Table 3.1: Male and Female Employment in Northern Ireland, 1984-87

|  | 1984 | | 1987 | | % |
|  | Males | Females | Males | Females | Female Change |
|---|---|---|---|---|---|
| Agriculture, Forestry, Fishing | 16,982 | 3,011 | 16,755 | 2,690 | -11.9 |
| Energy & Water | 7,942 | 1,181 | 7,171 | 1,154 | -2.3 |
| Manufacturing Industries | 70,155 | 38,246 | 65,572 | 38,130 | -0.3 |
| Construction | 25,705 | 2,238 | 23,495 | 2,267 | +1.2 |
| Services | 150,892 | 184,904 | 155,336 | 194,742 | +5.3 |
| All Sectors | 271,676 | 228,770 | 268,329 | 238,983 | +4.6 |

Source: DED, Census of Employment 1984 and 1987

Some of the growth in female employment is also accounted for by rises in part-time employment. Whereas part-time employment accounted for 21 per cent of total employment in 1984, this had grown to 24 per cent in 1987. The growth in part-time work has coincided with the rise of the service sector. The way that work is organised in this sector lends itself to a more flexible approach than in manufacturing where expensive plant and machinery must run for a specified number of hours. Part-time flexible working practices also mean cheaper labour costs. This has been encouraged by active inducement, through the tax and social security system, of low wage employment. For example, given an earnings threshold for paying tax and insurance of £41 a week, if an employer splits a 30 hour

(£80 a week) job into two with 15 hours (£40 a week) there would be a national insurance saving of £11.20 per week.  Given that the number of such jobs increased by more than one million in the United Kingdom during the 1980s, the total subsidy to employers of adopting such working systems would be in excess of £200 million per year (Deakin and Wilkinson, 1989).  Although the percentage change in Northern Ireland in part-time employment is the same for men and women, in actual numbers this meant an increase of 8,248 jobs for women compared to 2,755 for men (Table 3.2).

Table 3.2:  Growth in Part-time Employment, 1984-87 Northern Ireland

|         | 1984   | 1987   | % Change |
|---------|--------|--------|----------|
| Males   | 26,069 | 28,824 | +10.6    |
| Females | 81,452 | 89,700 | +10.1    |

Source:  DED, Census of Employment 1984 and 1987

The occupations and industries in which women work in Northern Ireland, differ from the rest of the United Kingdom.  This is related to the decline of traditional industries and the dominance of the public sector. Indeed, it has been argued that it is public sector dominance which has stifled the growth of private services particularly in the financial sector (NIEC, 1989).  The growth of these new industries in other regions has provided the stimulus for increased job opportunities for women (Table 3.3).

With regard to female employment in manufacturing, women in Northern Ireland are more clustered into the "light" manufacturing industries including textiles, clothing, paper products and food, drink and tobacco, than in the rest of the United Kingdom (See Table 3.4).  These industries have also been traditionally among the lowest paying, and the majority are covered by Wages Council Orders.

Table 3.3:  Female Service Sector Employment in the
United Kingdom, 1988

| Industry | England | Scotland | Wales | Northern Ireland |
|---|---|---|---|---|
| | Percentages of Total Employment | | | |
| Distribution Hotels Catering | 24 | 26 | 26 | 19 |
| Transport and Communication | 3 | 2 | 2 | 2 |
| Banking, Financial Services | 12 | 10 | 9 | 6 |
| Public Admininistration | 42 | 45 | 44 | 55 |

Source:  CSO, *Regional Trends*, 1989

Table 3.4:  Female Manufacturing Employment in the United
Kingdom, 1988

| Industry | England | Scotland | Wales | Northern Ireland |
|---|---|---|---|---|
| | Percentages in Total Employment | | | |
| Metals, Minerals, Chemicals | 1.9 | 1.0 | 2.2 | 0.7 |
| Metal Goods, Engineering | 4.8 | 4.0 | 4.7 | 2.6 |
| Other Manufacture | 8.7 | 9.4 | 9.9 | 12.6 |

Source:  CSO, *Regional Trends*, 1989

   This changing industrial structure has also altered the occupations of women.  By 1985, almost 70 per cent of working women in Northern Ireland were in only three occupational groups (a) professional and related in the education, welfare, and health professions, (b) clerical, (c) catering, cleaning, and other personal services (Trewsdale, 1987).
   As Northern Ireland moves into a post industrial phase, the economic activity of the future will be service-based.  Services whether to individuals, households, businesses, or communities will be the source of any new employment growth there is.  They will be smaller in scale than the giant manufacturing conglomerates, and they will demand a flexible,

well-trained, workforce. Women may well gradually move into a position where they make up the majority of employees in employment. What has to be ensured is that they receive a fair remuneration for their labour. At present, the picture is very complex with the earnings distribution becoming more elongated. This means that some professional women have secured highly paid jobs with status and stability, while others at the lower end of the labour market are seeing their earnings' potential decline.

## FEMALE EARNINGS - COMPARISONS AND DISTRIBUTIONS

### Distributions

The earnings structure in Northern Ireland has to some extent been determined by the changing industrial and occupational composition. The existence of such a large public sector where pay is negotiated nationally has possibly had the effect of boosting pay levels beyond what they would be if there was regional pay bargaining, or a larger private sector. This is especially the case for women: 93 per cent of females in public services in Northern Ireland are covered by a national agreement compared with 78 per cent in Great Britain (Harris, 1989). Undoubtedly too, the majority of the top decile of non-manual female earners in Northern Ireland whose pay was above £15,288 a year in 1989 were public sector professionals.

The following analysis of female earnings in Northern Ireland is based on data from the *New Earnings Survey*, 1989. This is a one per cent sample of all employees in Northern Ireland who were covered by PAYE schemes (approximately 4,100 were processed for the week including 12 April, 1989). The sample covers only those paying tax and national insurance contributions, and the absence from the data of those earning below the tax and national insurance thresholds must be taken into account especially when looking at female pay levels (since most part-time workers, and hence most of those earning below tax/national insurance thresholds, are women).

There is a wide gap between the earnings of manual and non-manual employees (Table 3.5). In addition, manual employees have to work longer hours to earn less money. Manual women have less opportunity to work overtime than manual men, both for occupational reasons and because of domestic commitments.

Table 3.5: Male and Female Earnings in Northern Ireland 1989
(Including Overtime)

|  | £ | % of earnings made up of overtime and bonus payments |
|---|---|---|
| Male Non-Manual | 288 | 9 |
| Male Manual | 181 | 17 |
| Female Manual | 125 | 6 |
| Female Non-Manual | 184 | 2 |

Source: DED, NES, 1989

Between 1979 and 1989, the divergence between manual and non-manual earnings has increased considerably (Table 3.6). Whilst this is particularly true for men, the increased difference between manual and non-manual women is also large (from 80 per cent in 1979 to 68 per cent in 1989).

Table 3.6: Divergence Between Manual and Non-Manual Earnings:
Average Weekly Manual Earnings as a % of Non-Manual Earnings
and £s Difference 1979-89

|  | 1979 | | 1989 | |
|---|---|---|---|---|
|  | % | £ | % | £ |
| Manual Males | 96 | 3 | 63 | 107 |
| Manual Females | 80 | 12 | 68 | 59 |

Source: DED, NES, 1979, 1989

This growing divergence in pay rates is reflected in the earnings distribution where the variance around the average is now considerable. Thus, there is a problem with using averages for an assessment of earnings distributions where a relatively small number of high earners can distort the figure by making it greater than is truly representative. A better indicator of the middle band of earners is the level of median earnings.

The median represents a line above and below which 50 per cent of all earnings lie. As Table 3.7 shows, median female manual earnings in 1989 were £115 per week (compared with an average of £125) while those of non-manual women were £158 (compared with an average of £184).

Table 3.7:  The Distribution of all Female Earnings 1989

| £ | Manual | Non-Manual | All |
|---|---|---|---|
| Gross Weekly Earnings | 125 | 184 | 168 |
| Lowest 10% Earned Less than | 82 | 98 | 90 |
| 50% Earned Less than | 115 | 158 | 144 |
| Top 10% Earned More than | 179 | 294 | 286 |

Source:  DED, NES, 1989

The Low Pay Unit has shown how little earnings distributions have changed in a hundred years. Figures on the distribution of manual earnings go back as far as 1886 (unfortunately they only cover male earnings). The lowest decile of manual men earned 69 per cent of the median while the top decile earned 143 per cent in 1986. The 1960s were the years when there was most equality inearnings:  then the lowest decile earned 70 per cent of the median and the top decile 145 per cent (Low Pay Unit, 1988). Table 3.8 shows that among women in Northern Ireland between 1979 and 1989 divergence between the lowest and top deciles has increased considerably and those in the lowest decile have dropped further behind the median.

Table 3.8:  The Differentials in All Female Earnings 1979-89

| | Lowest Decile as a % of Median | Top decile as a % of Median |
|---|---|---|
| 1979 Median £59.6 | 68 | 168 |
| 1989 Median £143.7 | 63 | 199 |

Source:  DED, NES, 1979 and 1989

Finally, the absence of many part-time workers from the NES (because they earn less than the tax/national insurance threshold) makes it difficult reliably to discuss the earnings of part-time workers. The limited data available from the NES suggests that the position of part-timers may have worsened over the decade. In 1979 women part-time workers in the NES earned 43 per cent of their full-time counterparts. By 1989 this had fallen to 37 per cent. (The average gross pay of part-time women in the NES was £58 per week.)

## Comparisons

The widening earnings inequality which has now been described for women in Northern Ireland can most clearly be seen when set against the background of female earnings in the rest of the United Kingdom. In 1989, manual women in Northern Ireland, along with those in Yorkshire, had the lowest earnings in all regions. Table 3.9 shows that even a declining region such as Merseyside and the North West, with similar economic problems to Northern Ireland - low GDP, high unemployment, and so on - achieved average manual female earnings of £135 per week in 1989, despite higher female unemployment rates (See also Department of Employment, 1989; Employment Gazette, October 1989).

Table 3.9:  Average Manual Female Earnings, United Kingdom, 1989

|  | £ |
| --- | --- |
| Highest-earning areas: | |
| City of London | 162 |
| South East including London | 149 |
| North West | 132 |
| Lowest-earning areas: | |
| Northern Ireland | 125 |
| Yorkshire and Humberside | 126 |
| North | 127 |

Source:  DE, NES, 1989 and DED, NES, 1989

In complete contrast to this, women doing non-manual work in Northern Ireland had the third highest earnings in regional terms (Table 3.10). This is clearly a result of the greater proportion of non-manual women in Northern Ireland compared with other areas of the United Kingdom, who work in the public sector.

Table 3.10:  Average Non-Manual Female Earnings in the United Kingdom, 1989

|  | £ |
|---|---|
| Highest-earning areas: | |
| City of London | 283 |
| South East including London | 219 |
| Northern Ireland | 184 |
| Lowest-earning areas: | |
| East Midlands | 173 |
| North | 174 |
| West Midlands | 178 |

Source:  DE, NES, 1989 and DED, NES, 1989

Despite government cut backs, employment in this sector shows only small signs of diminishing.  Whether or not there will be some expansion in the future, will depend on how far Ministers seek to attract more public sector work to Northern Ireland from the overheated regions in the South East of England.  (For a more extended and a somewhat different interpretation, See Chapter Two by Monica McWilliams.)

If there is a growing gap between different occupational groups of women within Northern Ireland, how do the earnings of different groups of women relate to those of their male counterparts?

In Northern Ireland the percentage difference between male and female earners is not as great as in other regions (Table 3.11). In Northern Ireland women earn 78 per cent of male hourly earnings compared with a figure of 76 per cent for Great Britain as a whole.  (Using hourly earnings for this comparison and excluding overtime gives a better indication of the real ratio of male to female earnings.)

Table 3.11:  Female as a Percentage of Male Hourly Earnings,
Great Britain and Northern Ireland, 1989

|  | Northern Ireland | Great Britain |
|---|---|---|
| (Excluding Overtime) | | |
| All Female Earnings | 78 | 76 |
| Manual Females | 78 | 71 |
| Non-Manual Females | 66 | 63 |

Source:  DE, NES, 1989 and DED, NES, 1989

There has been some improvement since 1979 when women earned
only 66 per cent of average male earnings (DED, 1979), but what clearly
emerges from such comparisons over time is that, although there is clearly
a widening gap between non-manual and manual women, the main change
in the last decade has been a particularly large increase in male non-
manual earnings (See Table 3.6).  This is probably a result of the growth
of new service industries particularly in the financial and business sector.

**Statutory Wage Fixing and Low Pay**

One of the oldest ways of protecting the earnings of the lowest paid
workers has been through the Wages Councils.  Their precursor, the Trade
Boards, were set up on a statutory basis in 1909 in response to agitation
against the growth of "sweated industries" dependent on female labour.
Despite the evidence that low paid workers still need this protection, the
Government now proposes total abolition of the Wages Council system.

While it is true that the industries covered by Wages Council Orders
remain low paid, there have been some improvements recently, with yearly
increases well above the rate of inflation.  This is largely the result of a
more active role by trade unionists in the negotiations.  For example, the
Catering Wages Council in Northern Ireland has recently set a statutory
minimum hourly rate of £2.56 which is a 9.5 per cent increase on the 1989
rate (Northern Ireland Office of Wages Councils, 1990).  This is still,
however, well below the hourly rate of £3.23, the European benchmark of
low pay.

Within Northern Ireland there are 36,000 workers covered by Wages
Councils, 64 per cent of whom are women.  Because the set rates are

legally enforceable, it means that the most vulnerable employees have a measure of protection against exploitation and underpayment. There is no evidence in industries where Wages Councils have been disbanded that the rate of pay improves, in fact the reverse is usually the case (Craig, 1980). The proposal to abolish Wages Councils within the United Kingdom has met with much criticism, not only from trade unions and welfare organisations, but also from the Confederation of British Industry (CBI) which fears that unrestrained competition would lead to undercutting of prices by disreputable firms, and worsen industrial relations generally (Gabriel and Palmer, 1984).

In Northern Ireland arguments against abolishing the Wages Councils have centred around the weakness of the regional economy, the high levels of unemployment and deprivation, and the lack of evidence to suggest that low pay brings down unemployment (See for example, CROW; ATGWU; EOCNI, 1989). These distinguishing features of Northern Ireland mean that if Wages Councils are disbanded in the province, the effect is likely to be more severe than in the rest of the United Kingdom.

## Campaigning for an Alternative:  Women and 1992

In terms of likely futures, the Single European Market must be considered. The impetus towards creating an integrated European economy arose out of the need to compete more effectively with America and Japan (Albert and Ball, 1983; Cecchini, 1987). The dismantling of barriers to allow the free movement of capital goods and labour is intended to allow the most successful companies, which are best able to make use of economies of scale, to become market leaders. In this process small and medium-sized companies with no export performance are unlikely to survive as independent entities beyond the year 2000 (NIEC/NESC, 1988; *Financial Times*, 20.2.1989). The Northern Ireland economy is dominated by such companies: 60 per cent of Northern Ireland companies trade only in the Northern Ireland market (NIEC/NESC, 1988). The peripheral location of Northern Ireland is also likely to be a major obstacle to success. There is little doubt that, as in America, industrial and economic concentration will consolidate itself in a few areas of Europe. These will be the industrial heartlands of Germany and the Benelux countries, Northern France, Southern England and Northern Italy. They have a number of key features in common: vast populations; large scale natural resources; centres of political and financial power; and international meeting points of transport and communication. Northern Ireland has none of these. Thus the changes in

Europe will be uneven in character, not only between the rich and poor regions, but within member States themselves.

A low wage economy such as Northern Ireland will not necessarily attract "new" industrial investment after 1992. 1992 may, however, mean that more skilled workers leave Northern Ireland. The doubling of the EC Structural Funds to poorer regions such as Northern Ireland is unlikely, therefore, to have a major impact unless there are incentives to retain skilled labour through higher wages, and to boost productivity through better training. At the moment, Structural Fund resources are only being channelled into infrastructural investment and existing social expenditure programmes (NIC-ICTU, 1990; NIEC, 1989).

There are two ways to try to begin to assess what the consequences of 1992 will be for women in Northern Ireland. On the demand side, we can look at the industries where women are concentrated and evaluate what the labour needs of those industries will be in the new situation. From a supply side point of view, it is the characteristics of women in the labour market which need to be examined.

To succeed, industries will be making changes to the way that work is organised, and demanding skills and levels of expertise in their workforces capable of adjusting to swift technological change. Manual occupations are set to decline as computerised operations replace the bulk of unskilled work. The growth areas will be in private service employment, and here management will be looking for a multi-skilled flexible workforce. A full-time, salaried staff will be likely to be employed as the core, doing work essential to the organisation, the rest of the work will be contracted out to to other companies or individuals working on a fixed contract basis. These are likely to be part-time and much of the work will be home-based. These trends are likely to be widespread throughout the Community, indeed 70 per cent of all new jobs created in the EC in 1989 were part-time (European Commission, 1989).

Can women as employees benefit from these changes? There is little doubt that employers in the newly expanding sectors regard women as ideal employees: they are adaptable to multi-skilled work, part-time and home-based work often suits them because of family responsibilities; and they are perceived as less militant than their male counterparts.

There are certain other factors working in favour of women, primarily demographic shifts which will mean far fewer young people in the labour market in most of Europe in the 1990s than ever before. This should give women extra leverage to pursue their claims for equal treatment, and better conditions of employment than they have previously enjoyed.  Professional women and those who are mobile will find their skills in demand across Europe, especially with the harmonisation of qualifications.  Northern Ireland is peculiar in this respect, having both the highest birthrate in Europe and the highest "A" level success rate in the United Kingdom (*Regional Trends*, 1987).  If new industries cannot be attracted to the province, then the brain drain and emigration of skilled women (and men) to other European cities is bound to increase.

The prospect of a single European market after 1992 has thus opened up new horizons and prospects for women's equality, but this will not be automatic nor a single linear development.  It is more likely to be piecemeal and slow especially at the legislative level.  And it may benefit some kinds of women rather more than others.  For those women at the bottom of the pay structure, the unskilled and those tied by family responsibilities, the prospects are quite bleak.  Their fate cannot be separated from that of the regional economy (Morrissey, 1989).  Dependency and inequality could be reinforced for those without proper employee status.  It is doubtful whether pay rates in Northern Ireland will improve, especially as part-time and fixed contract work be come more usual.  In this context, the proposals affecting women under the new European Social Charter offer the only promising avenue for change.

Under the Social Charter, the Commission is proposing a range of measures covering working conditions and basic legal protection which will provide workers in the United Kingdom with legal rights, in some areas for the first time (LRD, 1990).  The strongest of these will be the legally binding Directives.  Other proposals which do not have this weight are known as "Opinions" or "Recommendations" and, without consistent campaigning, these are unlikely to be implemented.

There is to be a new Directive on working time which stipulates a working week of not longer than 40 hours, although this may be calculated over a longer period to to allow for flexibility.  It is also includes a weekly rest period of two consecutive days, and the right to four weeks paid annual leave.  This would be very important for women working in lower paid manual jobs where annual leave is commonly restricted to two weeks.  The Commission is also proposing a Directive on contract employment covering non-standard forms of working.  This would give part-time and temporary workers the same rights regarding redundancy, unfair dismissal, holidays, and pay rates as their full-time colleagues.  However, a note of caution has recently been sounded by the Institute of Employment Rights, a labour law research body for the United Kingdom trade union movement.  In a recent report (Wedderburn, 1990) they argue that the Social

Charter will enhance individual rights for disadvantaged groups such as the disabled, women, young people and those on a typical contracts. But the broader collective rights, to bargain for wages, organise in trade unions and to strike will remain within the framework of national legislation under the principle of "subsidiarity". So while women will probably be the main beneficiaries of the Social Charter on an individual basis, the collective rights of employees as a whole will still be determined by the United Kingdom government.

United Kingdom Ministers have opposed or vetoed each of the Social Charter proposed directives. Some measures can be passed by majority voting at the Council of Ministers, (measures such as the Directives on working time, and on health and safety, look likely to be passed in this way) thereby avoiding British opposition. But others, such as the Directives on the rights of part-time workers, can still be vetoed under the old voting system. Important rights to childcare and training are not yet at the Directive stage but are only "Recommendations" which carry no legal requirement, and so can be ignored if national governments so wish.

## Summary

The evidence presented here suggests that the industrial and occupational recomposition accompanying economic change in Northern Ireland, has had a fundamental impact on the pattern of female employment and earnings. Non-manual, white-collar females have improved their position. They have increased their earnings, to maintain comparable earnings with similar groups in Great Britain, and achieved a greater proportion of male earnings. By no means have they achieved total equality with men but their position relative to manual females is substantially better than it used to be.

In contrast, manual women have fared very badly. They have failed to retain their earnings' level of a decade ago and are falling further behind all other groups of workers. If policy were based on rational assessments of progress or the lack of it, then this group would be prioritised within the general range of training programmes. It is most important to upgrade their skills, not only to strengthen their position regarding the single European market, but generally to upgrade their falling earnings performance. At the same time, the operation of public policy regarding the abolition of Wages Councils should be reconsidered.

The Single European Act offers contradictory possibilities. On the one hand, it will increase monopolisation and the underdevelopment of peripheralised regions (Becikover, 1989), while on the other it will offer significant opportunities to engage in new forms of politics at the European level. This is particularly the case for women where the battle to implement the Social Charter could crucially affect their conditions of employment and social support (Morrissey, 1989).

A lack of local political accountability and ten years of unresponsive central government have led campaigning groups in Northern Ireland to look towards Europe for a more positive response. There is now little doubt that the politics of economic and social rights for women will move forward into a European arena.

# REFERENCES

ADNETT N., (1989) *Labour Market Policy*, London:   Longman

ALBERT M. and BALL R., (1983) *Towards European Economic Recovery in the 1980s*, Brussels:   European Commission

AMALGAMATED TRANSPORT AND GENERAL WORKERS UNION, (1989) "Regional Secretary's Communication:   The Operation of Wages Councils and the New Wages Order", Belfast:   ATGWU

ARMSTRONG P., et al, (1984) *Capitalism Since World War Two*, London:   Fontana

BECIKOVER M., (1989) *Industrial Re-Structuring and European Community Responses*, Brussels:   Social Affairs Dept. of the European Commission

BLACKABY F., (1982) *Deindustrialisation*, London:   Wildwood

CECCHINI P., (1987) *The European Challenge. 1992 and the Benefits of the Single Market*, Brussels:   European Commission

CENTRAL STATISTICAL OFFICE, (1987, 1989) *Regional Trends*, London: HMSO

CENTRE FOR RESEARCH ON WOMEN, (1989) "Comments on Department of Employment - Wages Councils:   Consultative Document, and Wages Councils in Northern Ireland, note by Department of Economic Development", Coleraine:   University of Ulster Centre for Research on Women

CRAIG C., (1980) *Abolition and After - The Cutlery Wages Council*, Department of Employment Research Paper No 18, London:   HMSO

CRAIG C., et al, (1982) *Labour Market Structure Industrial Organisation and Low Pay*, Cambridge:   Cambridge University Press

DEAKIN S. and WILKINSON F., (1989) *Labour Law, Social Security and Economic Inequality*, London:   Institute of Employment Rights

DEPARTMENT OF ECONOMIC DEVELOPMENT, (NI) (1979, 1989) *New Earnings Survey*, Belfast:   HMSO

DEPARTMENT OF ECONOMIC DEVELOPMENT, (1984, 1987), *Census of Employment*, Belfast:   HMSO

DEPARTMENT OF ECONOMIC DEVELOPMENT, (1990) "Employees in Employment - December 1989", Statistics Notice, 9 March, Belfast: DED Statistics Research Branch

DEPARTMENT OF EMPLOYMENT, (1989) *New Earnings Survey*, London: Government Statistical Service

EQUAL OPPORTUNITIES COMMISSION, (1989) *Women and Men in Britain*, London: HMSO

EQUAL OPPORTUNITIES COMMISSION FOR NORTHERN IRELAND, (1989) *Comments of the EOC on Wages Councils: 1988 Consultative Document*, Belfast: EOCNI

EUROPEAN COMMISSION, (1989) *Employment in Europe*, Brussels: European Commission

EVASON E., (1978) *Family Poverty in Northern Ireland*, Belfast: Child Poverty Action Group

*FINANCIAL TIMES*, 7 March 1989

*FINANCIAL TIMES*, 20 February 1989

FREEMAN J., GAFFIKIN F. and MORRISSEY M., (1988) *Making the Economy Work*, Belfast: ATGWU

GABRIEL C. and PALMER S., (1984) "Wages Councils, Reform or Abolition", *Personnel Management*, February

GORZ A., (1982) *Farewell to the Working Class*, London: Verso

H M TREASURY, (1990) *Public Expenditure Estimates for Northern Ireland*, London: HMSO

HARRIS R., (1989) "Relative Earnings in Northern Ireland 1972-1982" in R. Jenkins (Ed), *Northern Ireland: Studies in Economic and Social Life*, Aldershot: Avebury, in association with the Economic and Social Research Council

LABOUR RESEARCH DEPARTMENT, (1990) *Social Europe*, London: LRD

LOW PAY UNIT, (1988) *Britain Can't Afford Low Pay*, London: LPU

MORRISSEY H., (1984) "Unemployment and the Northern Ireland State 1919-1939", Ulster Polytechnic Monograph: *The Other Crisis, Unemployment in Northern Ireland*, Jordanstown: University of Ulster at Jordanstown

MORRISSEY H., (1989) *Women in Ireland: The Impact of 1992*, Belfast: ATGWU

NORTHERN IRELAND COMMITTEE OF THE IRISH CONGRESS OF TRADE UNIONS, (1990) *The Implementation of the Single European Act 1992. A Trade Union Response*, Belfast: NIC-ICTU

NORTHERN IRELAND ECONOMIC COUNCIL, (1989) "Industrial Development Board for Northern Ireland: Selective Financial Assistance and Economic Development Policy", Report 79, Belfast: NIEC

NORTHERN IRELAND ECONOMIC COUNCIL/NATIONAL ECONOMIC AND SOCIAL COUNCIL, (1988) *Economic Implications for Northern Ireland and the Irish Republic of Recent Developments in the European Community*, Belfast: NIERC/NESC

NORTHERN IRELAND OFFICE OF WAGES COUNCILS, (1990) "Notice of
    New Wages Order", Belfast:  Northern Ireland Office of Wages Councils
NOVAK T., (1988) *Poverty and the State*, Milton Keynes:  Open University Press
POLICY PLANNING AND RESEARCH UNIT, (1984, 1989) *Northern Ireland
    Annual Abstract of Statistics*, Belfast:  PPRU
TOURAINE A., (1974) *The Post Industrial Society*, London: Wildwood
TREWSDALE J., (1987) *Womanpower No 4:  The Aftermath of Recession*,
    Belfast: EOCNI
WEDDERBURN LORD, (1990) *The Social Charter:  European Company and
    Employment:  An outlying agenda*, London:  Institute of Employment Rights

# CHAPTER FOUR


# WOMEN AND POVERTY

## EILEEN EVASON


## INTRODUCTION

Women and poverty is a deceptively simple title for an area of discussion
that stretches across complex theoretical issues, many areas for research
and difficult tactical problems. Accordingly this Chapter begins by first
reviewing definitions and measurement of poverty in general and the specific
issue of integrating women into this theoretical context; it then focuses on
the concept of independent access and the causes of poverty among women;
and finally looks at relevant policy changes focusing particularly on income
maintenance policy.

### Defining Poverty

The problem of defining and measuring poverty has been a central strand
in the study of social policy for decades. In the 1960s, Townsend proposed a complete shift away from a minimum, physical efficiency, subsis-
tence approach to a relative perspective and sought to develop methods of
measurement based on this in his massive survey published at the end of
the following decade (Townsend, 1979). We may call this approach scientific
objective relativism. It was criticised on a number of grounds: that it
failed to allow for taste or individual preference; that the data did not
clearly demonstrate the existence of a threshold dividing the poor from
everybody else (Piachaud, 1981); that it may not be possible to define
poverty objectively (Orshansky, 1969); and that the concept of relative
poverty is not "sellable" politically or socially. New ground was broken
by the development of the social consensus approach in the survey by
London Weekend Television (LWT) (Mack and Lansley, 1985). In essence
this approach argued that what constituted necessities of life should be

defined by reference to the views of the general population. In fact, the gap between Townsend and the consensus approach turned out to be more apparent than real in as much as the LWT survey (and subsequent similar data) suggested that the majority of the population perceives poverty as a relative state; and the threshold, or poverty line (established by the two sets of work respectively at 133 per cent and 150 per cent of supplementary benefit rates) were also fairly close. This came as something of a relief to those who for years had used a 140 per cent cut-off point. One outstanding difficulty with the consensus approach, however, is that people may lack some items considered generally to be necessities but enjoy others which are not. For this reason, Bradshaw's (1987) efforts to revive interest in "budget standards", that is, what can be purchased with set amounts of money - basing these on a relative approach - are of value.

I would draw two conclusions from these and allied developments. The first is that, as a pragmatist, I am concerned that emphasising differences rather than the degree of consensus which has emerged has political consequences for which the poor may bear the costs. Piachaud has warned of the possibility of the debate on definitions becoming "a semantic and statistical squabble...a discussion that is part of the problem rather than part of the solution" (Piachaud, 1987). We should note that these theoretical divisons were indeed seized on by government in 1985 in order to validate cuts and a restructuring of the benefits system based on concepts such as "targetting" and "efficiency" rather than "need" and "adequacy" (DHSS, 1985). As a feminist, however, I draw a second conclusion: I am equally concerned that women have been largely invisible in an academic debate that has gone on for nearly a century and the task of painting women into the picture, so to speak, poses formidable problems. It is, in fact, difficult to think of a task which more clearly exemplifies Pascall's proposition that:

> Feminist analysis is most obviously about putting women in where they have been left out, about keeping women on the stage rather than relegating them to the wings. But to do this suggests questions about the structures that have left women out; about the way academic disciplines work; about language, concepts, methods, approaches, and subject areas. Such a quest leads to a profound rethinking. (Pascall, 1986 p 1)

Moreover, bearing in mind my first conclusion and Desai's (1986, p 1) warning that "only those definitions of poverty which appeal to the widest possible audience will stick'', the tactical problems appear as substantial as the conceptual ones. Nevertheless, this task, I believe, is an essential one, as failure to build women into the debates on the definition, measurement and, to a lesser extent, the causes of poverty, has meant hardship for women; it has further meant policies which seem incapable of grappling directly with the problems they are supposed to address, and a lack of fit between our concepts and methods on the one hand and the world that women and men recognise themselves as inhabiting on the other.

### Defining Poverty: Whose Poverty?

With regard to definition, statements such as "their resources are so seriously below those commanded by the average" (Townsend, 1979 p 4) beg the crucially important question, "whose resources"? For women who are heads of household, this is not a problem but Continuous Household Survey (CHS) data show that at least half of all married women in Northern Ireland are not in paid employment (See Chapter Two), and as Pahl (1989) has noted, British law eschews the concept of community property and there is no legal requirement for a primary wage earner to share his/her earnings with the other spouse. Thus effective rights to maintenance only exist when the marriage has ceased. Family law is not, therefore, founded on an assumption that resources are pooled, commonly controlled and enjoyed, and the work of Wilson (1987) demonstrates that women - and men - are acutely aware of to whom the financial resources in a marriage really belong. Wilson noted that:

> For most of the women interviewed, men had the money and they had a share of it - how much or how that share was arrived at was something they preferred not to think about. (Wilson, 1987 p 141)

Failure to take account of this fundamental question means that current definitions of poverty wrap up together persons whose experiences, perceptions and entitlements and circumstances may vary enormously. As Glendinning and Millar, (1987 p 11) have noted:

> surprisingly, the incorporation into relative definitions of poverty of important social dimensions such as powerlessness have not been extended to any examination of the position of women and men.

At a minimum, definitions need, therefore, to distinguish between those whose access to resources is direct, formal and legal and those, principally non-earning married women, who may manage some or all of a household's income but whose access to resources is actually indirect and at the discretion of another person. The two experiences are clearly very different and the latter contains risks of poverty which have only recently begun to be examined. Research on single parents has long suggested a problem of hidden poverty amongst women and children in two parent families. Pahl, when interviewing women in a refuge, found that:

> many of them claimed to be financially better off since leaving their husbands. All were living on supplementary benefit (now, income support) receiving sums of money which represented the minimum amount on which anyone in Britain was expected to live. Yet on these meagre amounts they felt "better off". As I became sensitive to the implications of what the women were saying I started to ask about financial arrangements in the households from which they had come. It was clear that some of the husbands had had substantial incomes, but had kept so much for their own use that their wives and children lived in grim poverty; (Pahl, 1989 p 1)

and a survey of single parents in Northern Ireland noted that:

> for many of these women single parenthood represented a movement from poverty, as a result of the inequitable division of resources between husband and wife, to poverty, as a result of the lowness of benefits - not automatically, as is popularly supposed, from adequacy to penury. (Evason, 1980 p 22)

## Measuring Poverty

With regard to the measurement of poverty, the focus on the family, household, or tax/benefit unit, has meant that our methods assume, or at least imply, an equitable division of resources amongst family members and hence an equality of living standards between family members. However, Charles and Kerr's (1987) work, for example, on the allocation of something as basic and essential as food (which was the bedrock of early poverty research) suggests considerable inequality of living standards. At a minimum, we need more work of this kind looking at outputs in the form of aspects of living standards for different family members to complement the extensive data on inputs in the form of income. At the same time, we need to be aware that this more accurate focus is itself being overtaken by events. On the basis of British data, and looking at the position of all women, Glendinning and Millar have argued:

> the traditional position of the financially dependent woman now applies only to a very small minority - about 18 per cent - of all women...It can hardly be realistic, therefore, to ignore any longer the issue of women's independent access to resources (as conventional studies of poverty have done) on the grounds that this does not reflect their real total access. (Glendinning and Millar, 1987 p 19)

## Independent Access

The concept of independent access has a number of advantages. It offers an alternative for those of us who are as uneasy about classifying women on the basis of resources owned and controlled by others as we are about allocating women to this or that social class on the basis of their husbands' occupation. In my experience of working with women married to violent men of all social classes I have been struck by the fact that dependence is dependence is dependence. Statistics relating to income to which a person has independent access may thus come closer to conveying the reality of women's material position. For example, if we calculate the proportion of women living around the poverty line by reference to receipt of specific means-tested benefits (Family Credit, Income Support), we find that approximately 54 per cent of the adult female population and 50 per cent of men are living around the poverty line. But such an exercise obscures the experience of those women who do not have a right to "their" share of benefit payable or wages received. It also ignores the circumstances of women in households where income levels are above those giving entitlement.

Turning to income to which women have independent access, the picture is much clearer. We can quickly establish that the majority of women have no income or low incomes and are, I would argue, poor. On this basis, the female population divides up into three main groups. Firstly, non-working married women - some of whom are of working age and some of whom are retired. In Northern Ireland few women of retirement age are in receipt of pensions based on their own contributions, while most of those of working age will have no entitlement to any benefit in their own right (other than child benefit where there are dependent children). These women account for one-third of Northern Ireland's total adult female population. Secondly, there are roughly 230,000 married and single women in employment in Northern Ireland. One-third of these women are employed part-time. Using CHS data, we can classify 60 per cent of these as low-paid (that is, earning under £100 gross a week) workers. These women account for nearly one-quarter of the total adult female population. The third group of women are non-employed single women receiving benefits in their own right. Receipt of means-tested benefits (income support and housing benefit) by such women adds a further 17 per cent of the female population to our total. Note that no account is taken in this overview of women receiving national insurance benefits without means-tested additions, even though there will be many of these whose incomes are little above those on means-tested benefits. Nevertheless the total amounts to three-quarters of all women in Northern Ireland. That is, three-quarters of adult women in Northern Ireland do not have access in their own right to income above the level of means-tested benefits. The concept of independent access clearly, therefore, demonstrates the limited reward that women receive for their work: a consideration that leads us to the issue of explanations of poverty.

## Explaining Poverty

Fortunately there is now a substantial body of theoretical material on the construction of female poverty. Most of this material falls easily into the now dominant structural explanation of poverty. Interestingly, however, as late as 1978, Holman's apparently exhaustive analysis of the ways in which poverty may be explained contained not one reference to women's poverty as such (Holman, 1978). Theory has thus developed very rapidly in the 1980s and essentially locates the roots of female poverty in the general socio-economic position of women - namely in the division of labour between the sexes and the assumption that women are or should be dependent on and supported by men. This assumption dictates the rights and possibilities of all women, even though, as noted earlier, at any point in time only a minority of the female population may conform to this stereotype. Thus as Glendinning and Millar have noted:

> far from protecting women from poverty...women's assumed
> and actual dependence on men is in fact the major cause of
> poverty. (Glendinning and Millar, 1987 p 26)

The assumption and, indeed, prescription of dependence has four main consequences. Firstly it legitimates the channelling of resources from the state to the household via the male. The debates which have surrounded the two exceptions to this rule - child benefit and family credit - suggest that policy-makers are aware of the problem of the hidden poverty of women inside the household but only feel comfortable curtailing masculine control over resources when the issue can be overtly and emotively linked to child welfare. Apart from hidden poverty and the refusal of the state to build into its own structures the concept of marriage as a partnership, the resultant dependency for women can be offensive and damaging. The woman who is caring for a disabled husband may be astounded to learn that she is actually the dependant person; widows are exasperated that their benefits depend on their husbands' contributions and their own count for nothing. In addition, data indicating that the wives of unemployed males are likely to withdraw from employment come as little surprise to those of us who have observed the reactions of unemployed husbands, for example, when the impact of wives' earnings on their benefits is explained.

Secondly, the assumption of dependence legitimates a benefit system which fails to deal with the full range of contingencies which may produce poverty, and is limited in its capacity to deal effectively with those risks which are recognised. I shall look more closely at this later. Thirdly, as many have observed, the assumption of dependence legitimates the low wages paid to women as such, the treatment of women as a reserve army of labour, and was, of course, a major obstacle for decades in the way of equal pay legislation. Fourthly, it legitimates the assumption that women are and should be available to work on an unpaid basis in a wide variety of settings and, of course, this has a severe impact on opportunities with regard to paid employment.

The issue of unpaid labour deserves special attention in Northern Ireland, though of course this is a worldwide issue. Within Northern Ireland a number of factors suggest that the volume of unpaid work here deserves special priority in future research: larger families, for example, the higher incidence of disability and the significance of agriculture. Women's unpaid work falls under a number of headings. Husband/children and home care, and the care of the disabled and elderly, are the two areas most commonly focused on. We have little data on the first, though on the second a number of studies has demonstrated that informal welfare networks, held out by some as the lynchpin of community care policy, are very limited. In a small study of 100 mentally handicapped persons and their families a few years ago, for example, shared care even within the immediate family was a rarity, with the bulk of the burden of care in almost all cases falling on a woman (Evason, 1984). The area where we have least knowledge, however, relates to the unpaid work women do in small enterprises and on farms. The inadequacy of official statistics showing that only 0.2 per cent of women in Northern Ireland work in agriculture is indicated by a number of sources including the Northern Ireland Rural Action Project (See Chapter Eight). Reflection on this total volume of unpaid work suggests to me that if we cannot all agree that most women are poor, there can be little doubt that many are shortchanged.

**Future Policy**

Measures to resolve these inequalities are easily delineated but will be implemented only with great difficulty. The need is not simply to address the amendment of the social security system, but to resolve the problems of low pay and unpaid work and to consider the broader implications of current trends in social policy. These matters are now considered in turn.

With regard to low pay, the obvious options are minimum wages legislation, vigorous application of the principle of equal value and the expansion of day-care provision. All of these proposals as several of the Chapters of this volume show, have run into difficulty and are counter to the current philosophy of the government in office. Wages councils are being dismantled and the United Kingdom equal value provisions, as Patricia Maxwell has argued (See Chapter Five), are deliberately tortuous and unhelpful. In addition, whilst it was hoped that a government caught between neo-conservative family policies on the one hand and a growing shortage of labour on the other might change course on childcare, Bronagh Hinds' Chapter shows how, to date, ministers have placed responsibility for making such provision firmly on the shoulders of women and employers - despite the emphatic view of the latter that there is no prospect of industry making a substantial contribution.

With regard to unpaid work, the obvious options are an end to social policies which assume women will fill the gaps as the state withdraws from a variety of areas of care and a fairer division of labour within the home. On the question of women filling the gaps in welfare, whilst we tend to focus on the specific policy of community care there is a need for a broader analysis examining the ways in which the concepts now dominating social policy - the new macho managerialism in health and welfare - exploit and penalise women. So often policies concerned with value for money, increases in productivity - by reference to debatable performance indicators - and efficiency savings, result in a transfer of labour from poorly paid to unpaid women. The majority of those affected by competitive tendering for catering, laundry and cleaning services in the health service, for example, have been women who have lost their jobs or voluntarily accepted cuts in wages. Increasing productivity by raising throughput in hospital care means, in plain English, discharging people as soon as possible. Often we are not in practice treating people more rapidly but simply offloading part of the total care formerly provided in hospital onto the community, that is, women. The end of the traditional school meal also means that women must spend time (and money) compensating for the fact, for example, that their children now eat junk food in school cash cafeterias, or elsewhere, at lunchtime (Evason and Woods, 1989).

On the second question, that of achieving a fairer division of labour within the home, the problems here appear formidable and have been compounded by economic trends of the past ten years. Across the United Kingdom, rather than increasing production and productivity through investment, the trend has been to rely on fewer workers, with male employees doing more overtime and thus having less capacity to share in home and childcare.

With regard to broader trends in social policy, the consequences of moving towards the assumption that the state should have a residual role, and as far as possible there should be reliance on the private sector, deepen dependence and narrow the options of the poor generally and of women in particular. State provision has been crucial in providing women and children with access to services which relate to needs rather than to what wage earners can, or choose to, pay, and private market welfare theorists have never addressed the gender of the sturdy individuals they envisage buying whatever quantities of welfare they wish in the market place. In housing, the drive towards owner occupation and the end of the concept of the state as a general provider of housing - as opposed to a provider for special groups - has narrowed drastically the chances of women securing good accommodation in their own right. In education, as state schools decline and students in higher education receive less and less state support, how soon will it be before the issue of gender surfaces as parents make "choices" about the education of their children? In health care, in the move towards a two-tiered structure, with a thriving private sector for some and a poor quality National Health Service (NHS) for the rest, women will figure disproportionately in "the rest".

Turning specifically to social security, the problem of poverty amongst women has to be addressed at three levels: amendment or abolition of the insurance principle, a restructuring of pensions policy and a new approach to reduce women's disporportionate dependence on the means test.

The current operation of the concept of insurance in the benefit system is based on, and deepens the dependence of, married women. Insurance benefits are provided for a range of contingencies (sickness, disability, unemployment) with entitlement depending on the fulfilment of complex contribution conditions. The insurance principle can be seen as indirectly discriminatory as women, with their lower wages, broken career patterns and greater involvement in part-time work, are less likely to qualify for such benefits. In Northern Ireland, this problem is of particular concern since, as McWilliams has shown (See Chapter Two), women are less likely to be in employment than women in Great Britain, and increasing numbers of those who are in work are in part-time employment. It can, moreover, be noted that recent legislation has introduced stricter contribution conditions with regard to short-term benefits, hence current policy serves to exacerbate existing difficulties.

One obvious solution would be to simply abolish the contributory principle. My own view, however, is that the problems relate not to the principle itself but to the manipulation of contribution conditions to ration and limit access to benefits. If we assume claimants prefer entitlement based on the concept of contribution, then we could simply widen this so that contributions - obviously more progressively structured than at present - were paid by all employees (full- and part-time) and, extending the home responsibilities protection provisions, credit women with real contributions acceptable for all benefits for all periods spent caring for children or the disabled or elderly. This, along with an increase in child benefit and a more generous, accessible invalid care allowance, would build into our social security system real recognition of unpaid work.

For pensions, women outside the labour force could be credited with earnings. However, the problems here go much deeper. Pensions policies in the post-war period have been remarkable inasmuch as every White Paper has focused on the implications of this or that policy for the average male wage earner when, of course, the majority of pensioners are women. The problem of poverty amongst the elderly cannot be resolved until policies focus squarely on women. Worse still, recent policy developments indicate that the government's general strategy is to limit state provision in order to provide room for company and personal pensions schemes. Women will, by virtue of their poorer employment opportunities, do particularly badly out of this trend towards privatisation and the consequences are likely to be particularly serious in Northern Ireland. Pensioners here are already less likely to have occupational pensions than pensioners in Great Britain and those who do so are generally male. As a result, elderly women in Northern Ireland are much more likely than women elsewhere to be in poverty and claiming means-tested help. Thus, for example, in 1985, 80 per cent of elderly persons on supplementary benefit in Northern Ireland with no entitlement at all to a pension under the insurance scheme were women (PPRU, 1987). Moreover, even of those women entitled to a state insurance pension in their own right, 62 per cent still had incomes so low they had to claim means-tested help, compared with 19 per cent of single unmarried male claimants (*ibid*). For the United Kingdom as a whole and Northern Ireland in particular, there must be a reversion to the principle that provision for the elderly is primarily a state responsibility, that pensions should be adequate and that further provision is a matter for the individual. This means a reversion to State Earnings Related Pension Scheme (SERPS) in its original form with an increase in the proportion of earnings replaced and the assumption that all women will receive a pension based on their own actual or credited earnings.

Finally, there is the question of removing women from the means-test. In all EC countries it is noticeable that women have to resort to such aid to a greater extent than men. This issue can be addressed directly by extending the insurance structure through the adoption of what may be called the "principle of equal concern". There is an analogy here with the evolution of equal pay legislation. Equal pay for women doing the same work as men had little impact because women normally do women's work. The concept of equal value was a means of trying to correct this distortion. Similarly, in social security, giving women access to benefits on the same terms as men has little impact, partly because, as has already been noted, women are less able to meet the qualifying conditions attached to benefits. Often, however, the problem is that the benefits system is geared to those "risks" likely to be experienced by men. The risks to which women are subject have been discounted and hence women in poverty as a result of risks in women's lives, tend to be left to the least eligible part of the benefit system - means-tested assistance. The most obvious examples of this process are women who cannot work because they are caring full-time for the disabled and elderly, and single parents, apart from widows. The principle of equal concern would mean a reform of the benefit system so that within a new approach to insurance all risks were covered.

## Summary

This Chapter has sought to build women into the debates about the definition, measurement and causes of poverty. It has been suggested that the concept of independent access is an important step forward both in terms of research and in terms of future policy development. Using this concept it is clear that the vast majority of women are poor in Northern Ireland. A range of possible strategies for the future has been reviewed, but perhaps the most important of these is a change in the way we think about women in our theoretical discussions. The assumption of dependence, acknowledged or not, has had advantages for researchers and policy-makers. Life is easier when large numbers of people (women) can be bundled into larger units (households) and what actually happens within these units can be disregarded. The result of this strategy, however, is poverty for women and policies which fail directly to address need.

## REFERENCES

BRADSHAW J., et al, (1987) "Evaluating Adequacy: The Potential of Budget Standards", *Journal of Social Policy*, Vol 16, Part 2

CHARLES N. and KERR M., (1987) "Just the Way It Is: Gender and Age Differences in Family Food Consumption" in J. Brannen and G. Wilson (Eds), *Give and Take in Families*, London: Allen and Unwin

DEPARTMENT OF HEALTH AND SOCIAL SECURITY, (1985) *Reform of Social Security*, Vol 1, Cmnd 9517, London: HMSO

DESAI M., (1986) "Drawing the Line in Defining the Poverty Threshold" in P. Golding (Ed), *Excluding the Poor*, London: CPAG

EVASON E., (1980) *Just Me and the Kids*, Belfast: Equal Opportunities Commission Northern Ireland, p 22

EVASON E., (1984) *Who Cares: A Study of Mentally Handicapped Persons and their Families*, Northern Ireland: Triangle Housing Association

EVASON E. and WOODS R., (1989) "Poor Children, Poor Diet", *Health Education Journal*, 48 (1)

GLENDINNING C. and MILLAR J., (1987) *Women and Poverty in Britain*, Brighton: Wheatsheaf

HOLMAN R., (1978) *Poverty: Explorations of Social Deprivation*, Martin Robertson

MACK J. and LANSLEY S., (1985) *Poor Britain*, London: Allen and Unwin

ORSHANSKY M., (1969) "How Poverty is Measured", *Monthly Labor Review*, February

PAHL J., (1989) *Money and Marriage*, London: Macmillan

PASCALL G., (1986) *Social Policy: A Feminist Analysis*, Tavistock

PIACHAUD D., (1981) "Peter Townsend and the Holy Grail", *New Society*, 10 September

PIACHAUD D., (1987) "Problems in the Definition and Measurement of Poverty", *Journal of Social Policy*, Vol 16, Part 2

POLICY, PLANNING AND RESEARCH UNIT, (1987) *Northern Ireland Annual Abstract of Statistics*, Belfast: PPRU

TOWNSEND P., (1979) *Poverty in the United Kingdom: A Survey of Household Resources and Standards of Living*, Rickmansworth: Penguin

WILSON G., (1987) "Money and Marriage", in J. Brannen and G. Wilson (Eds), *Give and Take in Families*, London: Allen and Unwin

# CHAPTER FIVE

# EQUAL PAY LEGISLATION: PROBLEMS AND PROSPECTS

## PATRICIA MAXWELL

## INTRODUCTION

This Chapter examines recent progress towards equal pay for equal work, and in particular the development of the concept of equal pay for work of equal value, which was introduced in Northern Ireland in 1984. In this it builds upon and develops earlier work (Maxwell, 1989). The Chapter explains the background to the introduction of the equal value legislation and shows how it has been developed by recent case law in Northern Ireland. It seeks to highlight the numerous problems which have arisen, problems such as delays, expense, the inadequacies of remedies, the many procedural and technical difficulties. It examines some of the suggested solutions to these problems. It goes on to argue that in spite of its many imperfections, the equal value legislation is an important tool for instigating fundamental reevaluations of female-dominated work. Not only has it given rise to important victories for individual women in Northern Ireland, as highlighted in the Chapter, but it is having an ever-increasing indirect impact, as more and more employers recognise the need to seek to implement job evaluation schemes free from sex bias.

Almost 4,000 equal value applications have been made in the United Kingdom in the five years since the equal value law took effect in 1984. By 1990, barely 20 of these cases had been finally concluded; only one of these was in Northern Ireland. Significant but limited progress in respect of a number of cases was made in Northern Ireland during 1990, yet the impact of the equal value amendment to date has been disappointingly low, notwithstanding its enormous potential to bring about radical reappraisals of the work traditionally done by women. Given the complexities of the procedures, and the delays in obtaining a result, it comes as no surprise to discover that the number of new equal value applications is declining.  In the whole of the United Kingdom in 1988, only 140 applications were lodged with industrial tribunals.

## The Background to the Equal Value Amendment

It has been clear from the outset that the British Government was reluctant to introduce the concept of equal pay for work of equal value into British domestic law.  It did so only after successful infringement proceedings before the European Court of Justice in 1982.  The legislation clearly ran philosophically counter to the Conservative Government's aims of deregulation and free market competition.  The concept of equal value was merely grafted onto the existing legislation, which had been specifically designed to facilitate comparisons between jobs which were essentially similar.  The whole point and importance of equal value comparisons is that they are between jobs which are quite different in nature.  It is becoming increasingly evident that the legislative model of the Equal Pay Act (1970) is inappropriate for equal value comparisons.  The 1970 legislation aimed to eradicate wage discrimination in two situations:  where a woman was paid less than a man who was doing the same (or broadly similar) work; or where a woman's job scored the same as a man's under a job evaluation scheme voluntarily undertaken by her employer.  It is now generally accepted that the legislation was successful to a degree in removing these more blatant forms of pay discrimination, and resulted in a once and for all increase in female wages, relative to male.  As Trewsdale (1988) has shown, in 1973 women in Northern Ireland earned 63 per cent of male average hourly earnings.  By 1981, the figure had risen to its peak of 76 per cent;  by 1987, it had fallen back to 73.5 per cent.  The figures are significantly lower when gross earnings, including overtime and bonus payments are compared.  The trends in Northern Ireland reflect closely the picture in Great Britain.  If anything, the percentages in Northern Ireland are slightly higher, a fact attributable at least in part to the higher proportion of public sector workers.

Many reasons for the persistent pay differentials between men and women have been advanced, including women's generally poorer qualifications and more limited job experience; stereotypical attitudes and practices on the part of employers; and the traditional division of labour within the family.  Whatever is the case, the primary result is extensive gender segregation in the labour market (See Hakim, 1979 for Great Britain and Trewsdale, 1988 for Northern Ireland).  Despite the existence for many years of legislation specifically designed to promote open access to employment, the great majority of men and women today are employed on different work. Segregation is "horizontal", with women concentrated in certain occupations, which tend to be the least prestigious and lower paid. It is also "vertical", with women over-represented in the lower grades of work, and under-represented in the higher grades. There is evidence to suggest that at least some of this segregation resulted directly from the 1970 legislation on equal pay, as employers were given five years to comply, a period in which it was possible to restructure a workforce in such a way as to minimise potential equal pay claims, by ensuring that men and women did not do "like work" (See for example, Snell, 1979; Snell et al, 1981). The fact that the labour market was already so divided into "men's jobs" and "women's jobs" clearly restricted the number of "like work" comparisons which could be made under the 1970 legislation. By the early 1980s the number of equal pay claims before industrial tribunals had dwindled to a mere handful in both Northern Ireland and Great Britain. The legislation had become a spent force.

**Developments since 1981**

It was against this background that the infringement proceedings against the United Kingdom Government were brought by the European Commission. The ruling of the European Court (Commission of the European Communities v United Kingdom, Case 61/81, [1982] ICR 578), that the United Kingdom must implement the principle of equal pay for work of equal value, was hailed with great optimism by all those who wished to see a further erosion of the difference between men's and women's wages (cf Davies, 1987). The Government's intention to do no more than absolutely necessary to fulfil its obligations under European law, however, soon became apparent. The Government turned down the opportunity to rework the whole framework of equal pay law, preferring instead to add on to the existing legislation two sets of regulations, one substantive, one procedural amendments to the rules of the industrial tribunals. Instead of formulating equal value as the new generic concept, it was grafted on as a residual claim, only to be used as a last resort. The difficulties caused by the tortuous wording of these regulations are now legendary. Among the more recent criticisms is the view of the Northern Ireland Court of Appeal in *Tennants Textile (Colours) Ltd. v Todd* (1989) that the "rules of procedure are now very obscure and much too complicated".

Yet the initial optimism was not completely ill-founded.  The year 1989 saw two significant cases in Northern Ireland move further towards a favourable result.  In the first, a tribunal, for the first time in the United Kingdom, rejected the employer's argument that the existence of separate collective bargaining arrangements for a women and for her comparators should provide an automatic defence to an equal value claim.  In the second, a tribunal has refused to allow a Health Board in Northern Ireland simply to import wholesale the results of a job evaluation scheme carried out in England, without considering in detail its appropriateness to the jobs of ancillary workers in the Health Service in Northern Ireland.  These two cases are considered in turn below.

### Winton v Northern Ireland Electricity IT Case No 28/84

The applicant was employed in a clerical grade as an Assistant Mains Recorder.  She claimed her work was equal in value to that of a male Mains Recorder and a male Surveyor, both employed on manual grades.  Her claim was lodged in November, 1984.  In March 1985, a Belfast industrial tribunal ruled that the applicant had reasonable grounds for her claim, and appointed an independent expert.  In June 1987, his report was completed, concluding that the applicant's work was of higher value than that of the Mains Recorder, and lower value than that of the Surveyor.  There then followed an 11-day hearing, spread over seven months, on the issue whether to admit the report in evidence.  In June 1988, the tribunal decided to admit the report, and, at the end of a further three-day hearing at the end of August and beginning of September, ruled that the applicant's work was of equal value to that of the Mains Recorder, and of lesser value than the work of the male Surveyor.  The tribunal spent five more days in December on the issue of the employer's genuine material factor defence.  Northern Ireland Electricity (NIE) first tried to argue that the differential terms and conditions were due to the separate negotiating structures within which Mrs Winton and her comparators were employed.  The company carried on separate negotiations with different bodies representing the clerical grades (which were virtually all female) and the manual employees (virtually all male).  The company claimed that it was the relative collective bargaining strengths and achievements of these bodies which had led to the differential in terms and conditions.  The tribunal's rejection of this argument is one of the most important and far-reaching  aspects of the decision.  It stated:

> An employer may explain how sex discrimination has crept
> into his wage scales, if that be the case, by reference to the fact
> that he is negotiating with different bodies in respect of differ-
> ent classes of workers, but that does not, in the opinion of this
> Tribunal, amount to an excuse exonerating him from his re-
> sponsibility as an employer. (Unreported Industrial Tribunal
> decision, 11 May 1989)

In other words, the existence of separate collective bargaining arrangements for a woman and her comparators will not provide an employer with
an automatic defence to defeat an equal value claim. This appears to be
the first such ruling in the United Kingdom, and, if confirmed on this point
on appeal, will have considerable persuasive influence on a number of
similar cases currently pending in Great Britain, where female clerical
workers seek to compare themselves with male manual workers, each
group being represented by a different trade union.

NIE also argued that because of certain latent monetary benefits
enjoyed by Mrs Winton, such as flexi-leave, annual holidays, home-to-
office mileage and lunches, she was in fact over £400 per annum better
off than her comparator. In each case, however, the tribunal found the
comparison made by NIE to be flawed. For example, under annual holidays,
the employer had failed to take account of a term in the comparator's
contract which entitled him to take an additional sixteen roster days off
per annum. Similarly the employer had ignored a payment to the male
Mains Recorder, described as a "block grant", which aimed to compensate him for abnormal working conditions. The tribunal concluded that
the figures mentioned by the employer did not bear out the conclusions
which the company contended, and certainly did not suggest a balance in
favour of Mrs Winton in the matter of pay.

Finally, the employer argued that a work measurement scheme which
applied to the male comparator explained the difference in pay, and was
not related to sex. The tribunal accepted that a work measurement scheme
and performance levels indicated by it could, in an appropriate case, satisfy
the requirements of the genuine material factor defence. In this case,
however, the defence failed because only the comparator's performance
levels had been measured. If both the applicant and the comparator had
had their respective performance levels measured, the tribunal agreed that
it might have reached a quite different decision. The tribunal concluded
unanimously that the applicant was entitled to have her employment contract
modified, so that no term of the contract would be less favourable, in

terms of pay, than the male comparator's contract. The tribunal went on to award Mrs Winton arrears of pay for a period dating back two years before the claim was lodged, that is, to 30th November, 1982. Herein lies a problem. Although arrears for two years prior to the date of the commencement of the proceedings is the rule in successful equal pay cases, the equal value legislation is expressly not retrospective. Applicants can only be awarded arrears back to the date when the legislation came into force, that is, in Northern Ireland, to 15 March, 1984. There is a possible argument, yet to be tested in the Superior courts, that Article 119 of the Treaty of Rome, which contains no limitation of damages whatsoever, should apply directly. Under this argument, Mrs Winton might logically be entitled to arrears of pay dating back to November, 1980, the date she was first appointed to the post of Assistant Mains Recorder. This, however, has yet to be tested in the appellate courts, and the apparent inconsistency remains.

It is worth noting that the final decision of the tribunal was delivered on 1 May, 1989, almost exactly four and a half years after the originating application was lodged, so the case provides a striking illustration of the problem of delays which is discussed below. Nor is the story complete. It is understood that the company has lodged an appeal to the Northern Ireland Court of Appeal, and a hearing is pending. The final outcome of the case is awaited with great interest, not least by the electricity supply industry in Great Britain, where an estimated 25,000 clerical workers could be affected. The applicant was backed throughout her claim by her Union, APEX, and by the Equal Opportunities Commission for Northern Ireland (EOCNI). The significance of the case is that it is the first in the United Kingdom to go through the full tribunal equal value procedure, in which a woman in the clerical grades has successfully claimed her work to be of equal value to a man in the manual grades. Although the full amount of compensation has yet to be assessed, the result in this case could mean almost £2,000 per annum to many of these women.

## McAuley and others v Eastern Health and Social Services Board
## IT Case No 1/85 - 5/85

This case is not so far advanced. Five domestic assistants at Belfast's Royal Victoria Hospital, who are employed on grade I (the lowest grade) on the ancillary staff grading structure, are claiming that their jobs are equal in value to those of a male porter and groundsman, both employed on grade IV. This case is being supported by the EOCNI and by the women's Union, NUPE. This in itself is unusual, as NUPE in Great Britain has categorically refused to support industrial tribunal claims, and has actively discouraged its members from doing so. Equal value disputes are regarded by most unions as collective, or structural problems, rather than as individual ones, and the view of most unions is that collective bargaining is the principal procedure by which solutions can best be achieved. As Warwick (1988) explains, the strength of NUPE is heavily dependent upon its ability to bargain nationally, and individual industrial tribunal claims are seen as a route by which hostile employers might undercut national agreements. A perceived "knock-on" effect of individual successes is a return by employers to local bargaining, as a means of limiting obligations to improve pay. This approach of NUPE at national level has met with some grassroots opposition. Many members feel that a legitimate avenue of redress has been closed off to them. The policy of NUPE in Northern Ireland of supporting the women's claims, as part of a general strategy against low wages, is clearly exceptional.

In *McAuley*, the applicants lodged their claims in January, 1985. In December 1985, the tribunal ordered the appointment of an independent expert to assess the relative values of the men's and women's jobs. The Board then applied to stay the appointment of the expert, in order to argue a preliminary point under Section 1(6) of the Equal Pay Act (NI) 1970, as amended. This subsection provides an absolute defence to an employer, if he can show that he has in place a completed job evaluation scheme, which is analytical in nature (that is, it considers the demands made on the worker under various headings such as effort, skill, decision) and which can be demonstrated to be a scheme free of sex bias. Such a Job Evaluation Scheme has been described by the House of Lords (in *Leverton v Clwyd County Council*) as an employer's "most effective safeguard against oppressive equal value claims", offering him, "complete protection", in the view of Lord Bridge. An increasing number of employers are heeding this advice and implementing job evaluation schemes in order to "equal value proof" their wage structures. One such example comes from local government in Great Britain. The local government employers' representative body and the trade unions representing local government manual workers carried out a reevaluation exercise in 1986-87, which affected almost one million workers (4 per cent of the British labour force). This resulted in some "caring" jobs traditionally the preserve of women, improving their pay position by as much as 12 per cent (*Equal Opportunities Review*, 1987). Another example is the Midland Bank, employing some 50,000 staff in the United Kingdom which responded to the legislation and the results in some of the early cases, by introducing in 1987 an integrated job evaluation scheme, covering nearly all the bank's staff. This resulted in over 5,000 mainly female clerical staff being upgraded (Arthurs, 1989).

In the case considered here the Eastern Health and Social Services Board (EHSSB) argued that a National Health Service job evaluation scheme had been implemented by the Department of Health in London, and that under the principle of "parity" Health Service ancillary workers in Northern Ireland had been graded the same as their counterparts in corresponding jobs in the United Kingdom. Following 12 days of legal argument, spanning 1987 and 1988, a Belfast industrial tribunal in March 1989 finally rejected the employer's argument and confirmed the earlier order requiring an independent expert to prepare a report. The tribunal agreed that the job evaluation scheme in question was both analytical and free of sex bias. The issue was whether the scheme should extend to Health Service workers in Northern Ireland. The applicants argued that the Department of Health scheme should apply only in Great Britain since that Department had no jurisdiction in Northern Ireland. The ancillary workers' jobs in Northern Ireland had not been evaluated under demand headings. The Board had simply imported the results of a job evaluation scheme, but not the all-important means with which Section 1(6) is principally concerned. The tribunal accepted that there might be some distinctions between the jobs of ancillary workers in Northern Ireland and those of workers in Great Britain and ruled that the Board had failed to establish that any of the applicants' jobs or the comparators' jobs were ever evaluated under demand headings as required by Section 1(6). This case thus looks set to break all records in terms of the time taken to reach a conclusion. It has taken over four years to get a satisfactory result at a preliminary stage - the appointment of an independent expert. Given the procedural obstacles which still remain, the complexities of the grading structures involved, and the fact that the potential ramifications of the case are so far-reaching, it seems unlikely that a final conclusion will be achieved for some considerable time. Although the wider significance of the case cannot be properly assessed until a decision is forthcoming, the indications are that it will highlight the limitations of the "existing job evaluation" defence increasingly being pleaded by employers.

## Problems: Delays and Costs

One of the major problems with the equal value legislation has, of course, been the problem of delays. The legislation has now been in force in Northern Ireland for over six years. Only one case (*Tennants Textile (Colours) Ltd. v Todd*) has reached a final conclusion. The problem is particularly acute in Northern Ireland as there is a tendency to await the results of cases from Great Britain. But even there, the picture is scarcely more promising. Approximately 20 cases only have gone through the full procedure. On average each case has taken 16 and a half months from the issuing of a requirement to an independent expert to a final determination of the issue by a tribunal. There is evidence that this time is lengthening, and according to a survey in *Equal Opportunities Review* (1989) the average time in the last seven cases is 22 months. It is important not to underestimate the adverse impact which long delays can have upon cases. Women lose motivation for carrying on with the case. They may change jobs, or receive promotion, or face unpleasantness or outright victimisation from employers, reluctant comparators, or fellow-workers. As the case drags on, so the pressure mounts to withdraw the claim or settle for a compromise figure. In one extreme case in Northern Ireland, the firm closed down completely, rather, it seems, than face the consequences of fighting and perhaps losing the case. Although precise figures are not available, it seems that a high percentage of cases is withdrawn. The Labour Relations Agency (LRA) has criticised the delay, pointing out that it is not conducive to harmonious industrial relations to have a claim lingering on for years. The EOC in Great Britain has condemned the delays as unacceptable and in its 1989 consultative document reviewing the Equal Pay Legislation, put forward a number of options for speeding up the procedure (EOC, 1989).

The first option considered is to remove the jurisdiction of the tribunal and to refer equal value claims either to arbitration, or alternatively to an individual with suitable expertise, to perform a judicial function. The problem with arbitration is that it might be contrary to European Law, which requires that individuals have the right to submit claims to judicial process. The alternative solution is the one adopted currently in the Republic of Ireland, where Equality Officers, who act as officials of the Labour Court, determine equal pay claims. The system has some advantages, including informality, flexibility, low cost and speed, and many cases are completed well within 12 months. But the EOC expresses reservations: recommendations of Equality Officers can be difficult to challenge as they do not have the same obligation as an independent expert to produce a reasoned report.  It could also prove difficult to recruit people with the necessary legal skill and job evaluation expertise.  On balance, the EOC remains unconvinced by this option.

The second option considered is that of dispensing with the role of the independent expert, so that determination of the claim is left entirely to the tribunal.  This would clearly have the advantage of streamlining the system by removing the cumbersome three-stage procedure in equal value cases.  But there are disadvantages:  there is some evidence that the conclusions of the independent expert may lead to an early settlement in some cases.  There may also be some considerable advantage to a tribunal with little or no experience in job evaluation in having an independent and impartial adviser, particularly if faced with conflicting evidence from partisan experts produced by each side.  An alternative would be to use the independent expert simply as an adviser to the tribunal, but, in the view of the EOC, this would do little to improve the procedure.

The last option put forward is to retain the basis of the present system but to refine and improve it:  by ensuring greater availability of experts, perhaps by employing some on a full-time basis; by giving tribunals power to impose sanctions on both parties if they are guilty of unreasonable delay; by requiring the independent expert to give an explanation if the report is not produced within three months of the date of the reference; by improving rights of access to employers' premises for both the independent expert and any expert of the applicant; by replacing the "no reasonable grounds" hearing, which in at least two cases has run on for ten days, by a short pre-hearing review, to identify the issues and to determine the order of the proceedings.

A closely related factor which similarly deters women from making tribunal applications is cost.  The EOC in Great Britain estimates that a relatively straightforward equal value complaint resolved at tribunal level, including fees of counsel, solicitor, and job evaluation expert, will cost the applicant £7,500.  In the speech therapists case *(Clarke v Bexley Health Authority, Enderby v Frenchay Health Authority, Kelly Atherton v South Glamorgan Health Authority),* where hundreds of speech therapists have lodged claims for parity with clinical psychologists, costs of £60,000 were incurred, even before the tribunal decided whether to appoint an independent expert.  No legal aid is available in these cases, so without the financial support of the EOC or a trade union, there is virtually no possibility of commencing a case.  As we pointed out earlier, unions generally prefer to attempt to negotiate equal value settlements for their members, and regard tribunal actions as a last resort. The resources of the EOC are clearly limited. Women in Northern Ireland may be at an advantage, as the EOCNI has traditionally given a high priority to supporting individual cases, and has adopted a distinctly litigious stance, where a case raises any new point of legal principle, compared with its counterpart in Great Britain which in the past has preferred to operate at the level of exhortation.

### The "Individual Remedies" Problem

It is accepted by many people that the present reliance on individual proceedings to eliminate wage discrimination on grounds of sex is bound to be limited in effectiveness. The problem, as suggested above, is rarely in reality an individual rights issue. Rather it is a structural or collective issue. The Sex Discrimination legislation makes it unlawful to have discriminatory terms in collective agreements or pay structures, but there is presently no enforcement mechanism in the collective sense. The jurisdiction of the Industrial Court to review collective discrimination was removed by the Sex Discrimination (NI) Order 1988 (SI 1988/1303). This jurisdiction corresponded to that of the Central Arbitration Committee (CAC) in Great Britain which was removed by the Sex Discrimination Act 1986. The Industrial Court (unlike the CAC in Great Britain after *R v CAC ex p. Hy-Mac Limited* 1979) was able to deal with both direct and indirect discrimination in collective agreements. Since the removal of this jurisdiction in 1988, such agreements can only be challenged indirectly, by challenging those terms in individuals' contracts of employment which derive from the agreements. As we have seen, there are many problems facing actual and potential complainants, such as the deterioration in working relationships, the procedural complexities, delays and expense. In addition, even where an individual claim succeeds, the decision is not automatically extended to other women in a similar position. There is nothing to correspond to the "class action" of the American legal system. At present, where there are multiple claims in the United Kingdom, the tribunal may reach decisions on "representative claims" which will then determine the treatment of all other applicants. However, this can only occur where the parties to the proceedings agree, and such agreement is not always readily forthcoming from the employer. The only alternative is for every woman potentially affected to lodge an individual complaint, as was done in the speech therapists case. One measure which might obviate the need for multiple hearings, would be to empower the tribunal of its own motion to identify representative cases from amongst multiple applications, subject to consideration of the parties' views and a right of appeal.

## Independent Experts

Under the equal value legislation any case which gets through the preliminary hearing stage, must be referred by the tribunal to an independent expert. This is a unique experiment in the British legal system, and is as yet in its early stages. The expert is appointed by the tribunal and answerable to the tribunal, and in the case of Northern Ireland is drawn from a panel of seven men and women selected by the LRA. All the experts are part-time and come from a variety of backgrounds - employers, trade unionists, academics.

It has been suggested that it might be preferable to have full-time experts, as a measure to resolve the problem of lengthy delays, but there are fears that this might lead to a lower calibre of expert in terms of skill and experience, as the pay structure would not be commensurate with the current earnings of the panel. As Bowey (1989) has demonstrated, there is much that could be done to improve the present system. There is currently no formal provision for regular briefing and discussion sessions for the experts, at which recent cases and approaches to problems could be discussed, and inputs given from outside specialists. With such provision, the knowledge and experience gained by some could be shared among all the experts, and a body of "good practice" for judging equal value might develop. Bowey's study showed that there were a number of problems associated with the proceedings of industrial tribunals, including failure to provide the independent expert with adequate information to locate applicants and comparators, who might have moved house and changed jobs; failure to notify the expert to attend for cross-examination; and general lack of information on the progress of the case. Although experts generally received full cooperation with their requests to interview people and to have access to the workplace, this was not always the case, and more than one employer refused access to a former employee, who wished to demonstrate to the expert their skills in the workplace. McCartan's study in Northern Ireland (1988) suggests that use of independent experts can lengthen procedures by as much as two years. He also highlights the expert's lack of powers to deal with uncooperative employers and reluctant comparators, and the complete absence of such basic facilities as interview rooms, library and research resources, secretarial assistance, and so on.

The independent expert is given little statutory guidance on how to conduct the investigation into the relative values of the jobs. The legislation requires that the independent expert must act fairly and take no account of the difference of sex, but the expert is free to carry out the evaluation using whatever method believed to be appropriate. The procedure is based on the belief that it is possible rationally to determine the value of a person's work. The legislation gives little guidance other than to provide that the work of applicant and comparator be compared "in terms of the demands made...for instance under such headings as effort, skill and decision" (Equal Pay Act 1970, as amended, Section 1(2)C). The suggestion of various headings under which demands will be compared implies that an analytical approach is to be used, as confirmed by the English Court of Appeal in *Bromley v Quick* 1988. Bowey's (1989) analysis of experts' reports in 21 cases in Great Britain showed that every expert used at least three headings and none used more than ten. Factor weighting was not used. The factor headings chosen were very similar to those used in traditional job evaluation techniques. The six most common factors used by the independent experts were: physical effort, mental effort, skill and knowledge, working conditions, responsibility for things, responsibility for people. In traditional job evaluation the five factors most commonly used are: skill, responsibility, mental effort, physical effort, working conditions. Bowey's conclusion was that the independent experts had taken a fairly traditional approach to assessing the jobs, and in doing so, had not departed far from standard job evaluation practice.

But assessing equal value is different in at least three important respects from conventional job evaluation. Firstly, conventional job evaluation is constructed so that it replicates the "going rate" in the market. The market rate, however, does not necessarily reflect the demands of the job. Equal value assessments, in contrast, must ignore the market rate, which is likely to incorporate the results of years of past discrimination. (The market rate may be pleaded by the employer at a later stage in the proceedings as a material factor defence). Secondly, in conventional job evaluation the results are commonly designed in order to fit in closely with the existing pay structure, to maintain, rather than alter the *status quo*. Equal value assessments should take no account of the existing pay relationships or traditional differentials. Thirdly, there is the closely linked question of acceptability. This is an important test of a conventional job evaluation scheme, since its introduction is often the result of a need to replace a jungle of pay rates which have lost credibility, with a more rational structure. To be successful, the scheme must be accepted by the great majority of people affected by it, and must take account of considerations such as the relative bargaining strengths of different groups of workers involved. If it downgrades a group of workers in a strong bargaining position, it will be challenged and amended and its credibility damaged. The independent expert by contrast, is required to devise a method of comparing job values without the constraints of acceptability to the parties - by the very nature and existence of the proceedings the expert cannot hope to produce a scheme which will be acceptable to both sides. The only criterion for independent experts is that their evaluations must not be biased towards one sex or the other. The norms and conventions of traditional job evaluation cannot be assumed to be appropriate to equal value comparisons.

Arthurs (1988) suggests that the major problem with using independent experts for this type of exercise is that the results reflect the values of just one individual. He says:

> Job-evaluation-type techniques, however well carried out, are subjective, and are capable of producing a wide variety of results. In a full job evaluation exercise this hardly matters, since the relative values of different jobs can be based primarily on existing rank orders or upon the acceptability to all the parties involved. The independent expert is expected to ignore existing relative values and market rates, which may reflect inbuilt discrimination, and is unlikely to achieve a result which is acceptable to all parties. Therefore the results may be quite unpredictable, given that some experts will value particular job attributes more highly than others. (Arthurs, 1988 p 4)

The precise legal status of the expert's report has been considered recently by the Northern Ireland Court of Appeal. The case of *Tennants Textile (Colours) Ltd v Todd* was the first equal value case in Northern Ireland to be decided by an industrial tribunal. The case was appealed, and then returned for rehearing, and exemplifies many of the problems of equal value claims and in particular the role of the independent expert and the precise legal status of the report.

Proceedings commenced in June 1984, when a claim for equal pay was lodged by four female laboratory technicians who sought to compare their jobs with those of two male laboratory assistants who were paid £8 and £20 per week more. Originally the claim was under the "like work" provisions, but this argument was rejected in March 1985 by an industrial tribunal, which went on to hold that there was a *prima facie* case that the jobs were equal in value. In April 1985 an independent expert was appointed; her report, in the women's favour, was submitted in May 1986. The employer then sought an adjournment to facilitate preparation of his own expert's report. The hearing resumed in September 1985: the tribunal gave an oral decision in favour of the one remaining applicant. Some ten months later the tribunal delivered its written decision. This decision was challenged by the employer on the basis that too much weight had been attached to the independent expert's report. The tribunal had recorded that: the findings of fact were binding on both parties; the burden of proof was on the employer to persuade the tribunal to reject the report; and the report could only be rejected if the evidence was such that it was so plainly wrong that it could not be accepted.

The Northern Ireland Court of Appeal ruled that the tribunal had erred on all three counts. The burden of proving that work is of equal value rests with the applicant, and remains with her even when the independent expert has ruled in her favour. The precise status in law of the independent expert's report is of great practical importance, and this is the first appellate decision in the United Kingdom to consider that status in detail. The main thrust of Lord Lowry's judgement is that the expert's report is of less importance than had previously been thought. The report is simply evidence. There is no presumption that it should determine the case, or even that it should carry more weight than any other evidence put forward by the parties themselves. The tribunal is not limited to a supervisory function of ensuring that the independent expert did not act perversely. Its role is a judicial one - weighing all the evidence to determine whether work is of equal value. The Northern Ireland Court of Appeal clearly found difficulty with the procedural rules, finding them "very obscure and much too complicated", but concluded at the end of the day that too much weight had been attached to the report of the independent expert. The case was remitted to an industrial tribunal in July 1988. The tribunal which reheard the case was faced with two reports relating to the question of equal value: one from the independent expert, and one from the employer's expert, who disputed that the jobs were equal. Using the same five factor headings as the independent expert, the employer's expert assessed the comparator at the same score, but gave the applicant's job ten points - compared with the independent expert's assessment of 17 points - a considerable disparity. On the evidence, the tribunal preferred the report of the independent expert, for reasons such as her independent role in the proceedings, her greater experience and preparation. The claim was thus finally upheld, and compensation of over £6,000 paid out, almost six years after the commencement of proceedings.

## Permissible Comparisons

Another limitation of claims of equal pay under domestic legislation is that the male comparator must be in the "same employment", that is, employed by the same employer, in the same establishment.  Comparison with men at another establishment of the same employer is only permitted where "common terms and conditions of employment are observed", and provided that both establishments are within Northern Ireland.  This geographical limit (which applies also to comparisons with employees of "associated employers") withdraws much of the benefit of the legislation from women who work for Northern Irish firms which are subsidiaries of British (or Irish or foreign) companies, as they cannot make comparisons with workers outside the jurisdiction.  It also raises problems for home-workers, and for women who work in small firms.  It is interesting to note that there are no such limitations in the wording of Article 119, and some European countries, such as the Netherlands, allow for wider comparisons, something discussed by Szyszczak (1987).  Another recent decision of the Northern Ireland Court of Appeal, *Hasley v Fair Employment Agency* (1988), suggests that women who work for government agencies which are not technically "emanations of the Crown" may also be outside the ambit of the domestic legislation.  The Court of Appeal refused to allow a female office manager in the Fair Employment Agency (FEA) to compare herself with a man doing the same job in the EOCNI, who was graded two points above her, although the office he managed was considerably smaller.

## Concluding Remarks

There is considerable disappointment that the equal value amendment has been so slow to achieve any impact in Northern Ireland.  The decision of the European Court of Justice in 1982 was heralded as highly significant, in that the concept of equal value would allow comparisons between jobs which were quite different in nature, and thus allow progress beyond the impasse reached by the late 1970s.  With hindsight, it is difficult to resist the view that the British equal value legislation was specifically designed to minimise any such progress.  There is now a high degree of frustration and resentment on the part of women and their representatives as the complete unworkability of the legislation gradually manifests itself.

Increasingly people are turning to direct enforcement of European law as the only means to achieve a fair deal for women at work.

In a Northern Ireland context, it is difficult not to make comparison with new government initiatives to counteract religious and political discrimination in the Province. Largely due to American threats to withdraw investment, and pressure brought to bear by the Irish Government under the Anglo-Irish Agreement, strong new measures were implemented by the Fair Employment (NI) Act, 1989. These include monitoring the composition of the workforce, affirmative action, contract compliance and grant denial for employers who fail to meet their statutory obligations - the very measures long advocated by the sex, race and disability lobbies in both Great Britain and Northern Ireland. The Government is most reluctant to discuss the extension of these measures beyond the religio/political arena, preferring to confine the measures and depict them as of relevance only to Northern Ireland's "special" problems of sectarianism.

Yet it is important not to lose sight of the significance of the concept of equal value legislation as a tool to instigate fundamental reevaluations of female-dominated work. There is the potential through this concept to bring about radical reappraisals of the work traditionally done by women, and to give recognition to skills and responsibilities frequently overlooked or discounted. Northern Ireland has seen successful outcomes in a number of significant cases, such as *Winton* and *McAuley*.

It is important to remember also that the law is having an indirect impact in a number of ways: the considerable publicity which surrounds the cases has raised awareness of the issues, and generated recognition of the fact that a job may be under-valued because it is a "woman's job". In addition, a significant number of employers are now responding to equal value claims by introducing or re-designing job evaluation schemes free of bias against women. An example of such a scheme is that agreed by Eason and Sons (NI) Limited with the TGWU, following complaints by 14 female clerical workers that their jobs were of equal value to those of male warehouse personnel. It is encouraging to note that the EOCNI, in its thirteenth annual report, notes an increase in the number of employers coming forward for this type of advice and assistance. Given the complexities and defects of the legislation, this collective, joint approach, must surely be the way forward.

# REFERENCES

ARTHURS A., (1988) "Job Evaluation: The Impact of Equal Value", *Equal Opportunities International*, 17(6)

ARTHURS A., (1989) "Women Workers, Equal Value, and British Banks", in E. Meehan and P. Khan (Eds), *Equal Value/Comparable Worth in Britain and the United States*, London: Macmillan

BOWEY A., (1989) *Evaluation of the Role of Independent Experts in Equal Value Cases in Britain 1984-88*, Manchester: EOC

DAVIES P. L., (1987) "EEC Legislation, United Kingdom Legislative Policy and Industrial Relations", in P. McCrudden (Ed), *Women, Employment and European Equality Law*, London: Eclipse

EQUAL OPPORTUNITIES COMMISSION, (1989) *Equal Pay...Making It Work. Review of the Equal Pay Legislation*, Consultative Document, Manchester: EOC

*EQUAL OPPORTUNITIES REVIEW*, (1987) "Local Authorities' Job Evaluation", May/June

*EQUAL OPPORTUNITIES REVIEW*, (1989) "Equal Value Update", July/August

HAKIM C., (1979) *Occupational Segregation*, Research Paper No 9, London: Department of Employment

MAXWELL P., (1989) "The Impact of Equal Value Legislation in Northern Ireland", *Policy and Politics*, 17(4)

McCARTAN P., (1988) "Equal Pay for Work of Equal Value: The Northern Ireland Experience So Far", Unpublished MSc Thesis, University of Ulster at Jordanstown

SNELL M., (1979), "The Equal Pay and Sex Discrimination Acts: their Impact in the Workplace", *Feminist Review*, 1

SNELL M., GLUCKLICH P. and POVALL M., (1981) "Equal Pay and Opportunities", Research Paper No 20, London: Department of Employment

SZYSZCZAK E., (1987) "The Equal Pay Directive and United Kingdom Law", in C. McCrudden (Ed), *Women, Employment and European Equality Law*, London: Eclipse

TREWSDALE J.,(1988) *Womanpower No 4: The Aftermath of the Recession*, Belfast: EOCNI

WARWICK L., (1988) "British Unions and Equal Pay", Unpublished Paper presented at University of Bath, December, 1988

# CHAPTER SIX

# CHILDCARE PROVISION AND POLICY

## BRONAGH HINDS

## INTRODUCTION

The looming shortage of labour for the United Kingdom economy has led the Government to begin to reexamine the role of childcare as a means of permitting women to join or remain in the workforce. The budget of March 1990 gave formal recognition to this by ceasing to regard some childcare provided by employers as a taxable benefit. Overall, however, there is still little commitment to providing public funds for the large expansion needed in childcare facilities; instead the Government is looking to community groups, charities and employers to relieve mothers of the burden of childcare. Moreover, official policies remain uncoordinated and sometimes contradictory, often motivated by quite different philosophies

This has been well known for years to individuals and organisations campaigning for improved services. The deficiencies were openly recognised in Northern Ireland more than a decade ago, when a Government White Paper admitted that there was a very low level of services for under fives (DHSS/DENI, 1978). The improvements promised then have been scaled down and progress has been hampered by expenditure cuts, antiquated attitudes and a failure of the key Government Departments - Health, Education and Economic Development - to work properly with one another or with the voluntary sector.

A European Communities report in 1988, coordinated by Peter Moss, showed that the United Kingdom, Ireland and the Netherlands had the lowest levels of publicly-funded childcare services in the EC for children of all ages. Within the United Kingdom, Northern Ireland was found to have the worst provision by far, all the evidence indicating that it was the most disadvantaged area of the EC in relation to childcare (Moss, 1988).

This Chapter reviews the impact of childcare provision (or lack of it) on women's employment, highlights the inadequacies of childcare services in Northern Ireland, and argues that policy on the subject has been narrowly focused, serving to stigmatise the users of childcare by concentrating on children "at risk" and "in need". It proposes an alternative approach which could ensure that children are properly cared for and that women are freed to fill jobs that will otherwise remain vacant.

## Childcare and Work

> Childcare is a key issue for the Community both in ensuring
> its availability, if the economy is not to experience serious
> skill and labour market shortages, and its quality, to ensure
> that it provides a positive experience for Europe's children.
> (Cohen, 1989 p 3)

Inadequate childcare reduces women's opportunities to undertake education and training; it limits their ability to go out to work, and, even if available, it can restrict the number of hours women are able to work and the nature of the work women do. For women in employment, the absence of adequate childcare often forces them to leave when children are born, or to move from full-time to part-time work, thus reducing their earnings, promotion prospects and benefits such as pensions.

Joshi (1987), using data from Great Britain, calculated that a woman on average earnings, taking an eight-year break from work in her late 20s to look after two children, would lose £135,000 during her lifetime compared with a woman with no children. She attributed 40 per cent of the loss to being out of employment and 40 per cent to shorter working hours on return. The rest is due to lower pay after returning, some of which is attributable to loss of work experience while out of the labour force. The sum of £135,000 excludes loss of pension and other entitlements. Many women, therefore, pay for childcare by foregoing income. Women pay in another sense, in that they make up the large workforce of low-paid childminders and care workers. Since they depend on low-paid women workers for their pay, the vicious circle of low-income women is perpetuated.

Annual reports on the *British Social Attitudes Surveys* show that it is still overwhelmingly the case that the woman is responsible for looking after the home. Even where both partners work full-time, the domestic tasks are done mainly by women in 72 per cent of cases and shared equally in only 22 per cent (Witherspoon, 1985). Likewise, women largely shoulder the burden of childcare. It is women who set up childcare arrangements, women who leave and collect children and women who arrange the finances.

One factor perpetuating the unshared nature of childcare and domestic work between men and women is that fathers spend longer hours in paid work than mothers. Very few work less than 30 hours per week and many work more than 50. Moss (1988) found that nearly a third of employed fathers worked 50 or more hours weekly and that the difference between the work hours of employed mothers and fathers is largest in the United Kingdom and the Netherlands - two of the worst childcare providers. He also pointed out that in the United Kingdom, high levels of unemployment co-exist alongside long working hours for the employed.

There is a clear link between the adequacy of childcare and the numbers of women working. Moss (1988) found that only in Denmark did employment rates for mothers come near those for fathers. In Denmark the difference is 17 per cent, whereas in the EC as a whole it ranged from 40 per cent to 70 per cent; this in a country where employment rates for men are higher than elsewhere. Denmark also has by far the best provision of childcare in the Community and caters specifically for the needs of working parents. Moreover, the proportion of its gross national product spent on publicly-funded childcare for the under fives is six times that spent in the United Kingdom. The employment participation rate of mothers with children under five is lower in the United Kingdom, Ireland and the Netherlands than in all other member States. These countries are also the worst providers of childcare. The United Kingdom rate of 28 per cent is among the lowest in the industrialised world generally, substantially lower, for example, than in the United States or Canada (Moss, 1988). Furthermore, the United Kingdom is the only exception to the EC pattern that employment rates for mothers with children aged five or more are generally similar to those for mothers with younger children. In both Great Britain and Northern Ireland, only 28 per cent of mothers with under-fives were in paid employment, while this was true of 58 per cent of mothers of five-ten year olds and 69 per cent of mothers with children aged 11-15 in Great Britain (Cohen, 1988). In Northern Ireland, the proportions of working mothers with children in the two older age groups were lower, 45 per cent and 58 per cent respectively (Cohen, 1988; See also Chapter Two).

In the United Kingdom, the pattern has been that most women work full-time up until the birth of their first child; take a break from work and then take part-time jobs when they return. As a result, "by far the largest component of Britain's part-time labour force are married women with children" (Hurstfield cited in Moss, 1987 p 17). Four-fifths of women in the United Kingdom leave work after the birth of their first child, some returning later. Only three per cent remain in the labour market throughout their childbearing years (Martin and Roberts, 1984). By contrast, in Denmark, most women remain in the workforce and in France more than a third do so.

In most EC countries, most employed mothers have full-time jobs, and in two countries full-time and part-time working mothers are approximately equal in numbers. The United Kingdom is one of only two countries in which working mothers are much more likely to be part-time than full-time. Most mothers in the United Kingdom are employed less than 30 hours per week; between 15 per cent and 30 per cent work fewer than 20 hours and many work less than ten hours per week. The United Kingdom has 40 per cent of all part-time workers in the EC (Moss, 1988).

This large army of part-time workers is a major point of concern for women, especially for those with children. Most are poorly paid, four out of every five earning less than the Council of Europe's decency threshold of £3.25 per hour. Many are not covered by statutory employment rights. The Government is considering reducing further those rights that do exist for those working less than 20 hours per week, something which will affect half the working mothers with children under five.

Provision of other forms of support for women and families is also poor and often lags behind other European countries. Maternity provision, for example, is on a different basis from all other member States. There is no statutory maternity leave as such, but rather, under certain circumstances, a right to stop work and a right to return to work. This provision offers potentially longer (29 weeks) absence from work for women than do maternity leave arrangements in other EC countries. There are, however, more qualifying conditions attached to this absence than there are to leave arrangements elsewhere, and more of this absence is at the woman's own expense. Only during the first six weeks of absence in the United Kingdom is statutory maternity pay, based on previous earnings, available. Thereafter, half the absence is covered by a low-level flat-rate weekly payment, and in the remaining half no income is available to the woman on a statutory basis. In addition, the United Kingdom makes no provision for parental leave, that is, leave for fathers as well as for mothers. Six countries in the EC already have parental leave provision; two are considering introducing it; and two have other leave arrangements which cover parental leave. The United Kingdom, by contrast, has been the major block to the implementation of an EC Directive on Parental Leave. The absence of parental leave together with poor maternity provision and subsequently low levels of childcare provision, must lead to the view that in the United Kingdom, the system is essentially one of unpaid childcare leave for women, a system which promotes traditional patterns of domestic responsibility once a reasonable period for childbirth and maternal health has ended.

The general lack of support for women and young families in the United Kingdom has a particular effect on lone parent families (the vast majority of which are headed by women). In most European countries, the number of lone parent households is increasing, being highest in the United Kingdom, Denmark and Germany. The United Kingdom is one of three countries in the EC where employment rates are lower for lone mothers with children under the age of ten than they are for mothers with partners (Moss, 1988).

Lone parents have special needs. Without the financial contribution of another adult, they cannot afford less than full-time work; and hence require whole daycare facilities and financial support. In April 1988, the United Kingdom Government reduced substantially its contribution to lone parents taking up job opportunities by removing their right to a disregard for childcare costs in calculating benefits. Yet in January 1989, the *Guardian* drew attention to Ministerial comments about the State having to "foot the bill for the so-called dependency culture"; it reported Government plans to review the circumstances of single parents who received benefits in a sample of one out of every ten benefit offices to determine why they were not working (*Guardian*, 18.1.1989). An examination of policies and provision in other EC countries in relation to childcare and support for working mothers and fathers in general, as well as policies relating to lone parents in particular, might have given a better indication of why these parents find it difficult to work.

Despite low levels of childcare provision and a general lack of support for families in fiscal and social policy, the United Kingdom Government is encouraging women to return to work. This is not prompted by a new commitment to equality, but by the demographic decline, specifically the need to compensate for the declining number of schoolleavers to fill vacancies in the labour force. In this context, the Department of Employment has forecast that an additional 900,000 women will be needed in the labour force in Great Britain by the year 2000 (*Employment Gazette*, April 1989). Since the number of young women leaving school is also falling, it is expected that most of the increase in women workers will be from the 25-55 age group. The impact of this change is already being seen. In the year ending September 1989, the number of male employees in Great Britain fell by 14,000, whereas the number of female employees rose by 218,000, precisely half of them in part-time jobs (Training Agency, 1990). The female labour force is expected to increase in all regions in Great Britain, including those with relatively high levels of unemployment. It is likely that some at least of this effect will be seen in Northern Ireland where, despite high male unemployment, some industries and occupations which traditionally rely on women's labour have been experiencing shortages (See for example, NITA, 1988; Maguire and Ward, 1989 on the clothing industry). The Industrial Development Board (IDB) in Northern Ireland has noted:

> The problem is that many employers harbour negative attitudes towards those members of the workforce who are most able to bridge their labour and skills gap - women. Yet so far, very few employers have made serious attempts to maintain contact or offer training to their former female employees who have taken a career break to raise children. Moreover the provision of nursery care in the United Kingdom is amongst the lowest in the EC. In most parts of Great Britain it is very hard for mothers with pre-school children who wish to work to find public care facilities. Workplace-based creches are also very rare. (IDB, 1989 p 5)

This Section has argued that inadequate childcare has for years prevented women from going out to work even if they wanted to. Now that the wishes of women, the needs of the labour market and the promptings of the Government are all in the same direction, the time is opportune to make rapid progress. The material below, however, shows that there is a great deal to be done in terms of providing resources and changing attitudes.

## Childcare in Northern Ireland

Northern Ireland is an area of economic and social disadvantage in the United Kingdom and in the EC as a whole. Northern Ireland, the Republic of Ireland, Greece, Portugal, Corsica, parts of Spain and Southern Italy are Objective One regions for the purposes of the EC Structural Funds, because of their low level of development and high level of disadvantage. Within this economically and socially disadvantaged area, there are some 300,000 households, of which about 120,000 contain children. There are approximately 135,000 under-fives, 152,000 aged five-ten and 435,000 children altogether.

While the United Kingdom has the worst record for childcare provision in the EC, Northern Ireland has by far the worst level of provision in the United Kingdom. During the Second World War, as in Great Britain, State nurseries were opened to encourage women to enter the factories and offices left empty by men at war. In Northern Ireland, all of these were shut when emergency female labour was no longer required (McShane, 1987). The 1960s and 1970s were periods of considerable social change which produced a more favourable climate for the development of childcare services (EHSSB, 1987). Pre-school provision received a considerable boost from the Ministry of Community Relations, which funded playgroups in areas of social need in the early 1970s. In 1976-77, further funding provided another boost to the creation of playgroups in areas of special need. As in other countries, the injection of resources coupled with a progressive policy brought to light a substantial demand for childcare facilities. However, the level of provision, especially by public authorites, remained extremely low, a fact that was admitted in a White Paper produced by a joint Department of Health and Social Services and Department of Education Review Group in 1978 (DHSS/DENI, 1978). The present situation in relation to five forms of provision is considered below.

*Nursery Education*

The result of four decades of low provision is that today Northern Ireland's under-fives are less likely to receive nursery education than their counterparts in the rest of the United Kingdom. In 1985, for example, Northern Ireland had 7,025 pupils in the nursery sector; this is a ratio of 130 per 1000 children compared with 233 per 1000 in Great Britain (Cohen, 1988). The concern for parity with Great Britain which has influenced many other areas of social and economic policy in Northern Ireland (Bradshaw, 1989) has not, it seems, had any effect on the opportunities for pre-school children in Northern Ireland. The latest figures available show that in January 1987 there were 7,108 three and four year olds in nursery schools and classes in Northern Ireland, compared with 6,533 five years earlier. This growth however disguises a decline in the number of children attending nursery education full-time, from 4,753 in 1982 to 4,353 in 1987 (DENI, 1988).

The figures also show that many more under-fives were attending primary schools full-time than were at nursery schools or classes. In January 1987, there were 16,965 under-fives in primary schools (as well as 231 in preparatory and 87 in special schools); this means about one-third of three- and four-year olds were in primary school, making this sector, in effect, the largest provider of places for the under-fives.

Deep concern has existed for many years among those working in the childcare field about the large number of under-fives in primary school in Northern Ireland, especially since 1,484 of those attending were only three years old (*ibid*). In their submission to a discussion paper issued by DHSS/DENI in 1977 on daycare and education for the under-fives, voluntary groups argued that the enrolment of pupils before the minimum statutory age militates against adequate pre-school provision and that the children are not adequately catered for in staffing, curriculum content, environment and ethos (Hinds, 1985). A recent Select Committee report expressed its reservations in the following way:

> In its consideration of the current situation and pattern of provision, the Committee's greatest area of concern has been the admission of under fives to primary schools. There is much evidence - and we have learnt much about this during our own visits - that the provision made in reception classes for under fives is not of an appropriate quality. This concern has been shared by many witnesses and cited in a large number of submissions. (Education, Science and Arts Committee 1988, p xxxii)

It is reasonable to assume that many parents would choose nursery education rather than primary education for their under-fives if places were available. The shortfall of nursery places is substantial and has not improved significantly in recent years. In 1974, DENI set a target of 18,000 nursery places to be achieved within ten years. Adequate finance was not allocated to make this a reality and actual provision fell far behind the target. The DHSS/DENI policy statement in 1978 set a new, reduced target of 8,350 new places by 1983 (DHSS/DENI, 1978). In 1987 - four years after the target date - Northern Ireland was still several thousand places adrift of the reduced target, with a total of only 4,353 full-time and 2,755 part-time places in nursery classes and schools (DENI, 1988).

While provision in the 1980s has been poor, prospects for the 1990s appear even more grim. In 1982, the Government removed from DENI and the Education and Library Boards the legal duty to provide nursery education. This had severe consequences for pre-school children at a time of financial cutbacks, since they had to go to the back of the queue behind statutory services for funds. The policy of DENI remains that it is committed to providing nursery education, but that at a time of restricted public expenditure, priority must be given to children of compulsory school age. This does not augur well for nursery provision. As the Chair of one Education and Library Board said in 1983:

> Nursery schools are over and above our optional requirement so I fear that they could be hit when we sit down to discuss the budget for 1984-85. (*Ulster Newsletter*, 2.3.1983)

Mr Gerry Moag, Chief Officer of the Belfast Education and Library Board (BELB), wrote in October 1985 to the Department of Education on the need to cut non-statutory areas of the Board's activities by £1.7m as follows: "This must mean the termination or major reduction of services such as nursery education..." (Hinds, 1985 p 7).

The select committee report referred to above commented of England and Wales that:

> it should be the objective of both central and local government to ensure the steady expansion of provision of nursery education until it is available to all three and four year old children whose parents desire it for them. (Education, Science and Arts Committee 1988 p xiv)

This echoes the 1978 White Paper in Northern Ireland (DHSS/DENI, 1978), and applies with particular force because of the large proportion of three- and four-year olds being catered for in primary schools and the large degree of social deprivation officially recognised by the EC.

In fact, policy is going in the opposite direction. Instead of increasing the number of places for nursery pupils, the Government has decided to lower the compulsory school age from five to four. The practical effect is that from September 1990 onwards, pupils will be expected to attend primary school if they have reached the age of four years and two months (Education Reform (NI) Order 1989, Article 156). This has been done without any public discussion as to the suitability for children of this age of the Common Curriculum which has been introduced by the same Order.

Indeed, few parents seemed aware of the change until the Government distributed to all homes a booklet announcing it (DENI, 1990a).

## Playgroup Provision

Low levels of provision in the nursery school sector have not been compensated for by high levels of other provision for pre-school children in Northern Ireland. The DHSS/DENI joint review noted that in 1978 there were 7,190 playgroup places in Northern Ireland, of which 3,800 were in the Eastern Health and Social Services Board (EHSSB) area, 1,345 in the Northern Health and Social Services Board (NHSSB), 1,365 in the Western Health and Social Services Board (WHSSB) and only 680 in the Southern Health and Social Services Board (SHSSB). It aimed to double the number of places within five years, creating a target of 14,500 places in playgroups and family daycentres (DHSS/DENI, 1978). In 1985, this target had still not been reached, and only 11,224 playgroup places existed. This represented 208 places per 1000 children aged three and four compared with the United Kingdom average of 322, a substantial shortfall (Cohen, 1988). The latest statistics from the DHSS indicate that in 1988 the number of playgroup places had risen to 13,206, but this was still short of the target set a decade earlier; the average of 244 places per 1000 children remained well below the level of provision in Great Britain (DHSS, 1990).

Even if levels of provision in primary schools, nursery schools and playgroups were to rise in the 1990s, such provision would not necessarily on its own provide adequate childcare for working parents. Playgroups in particular have such short hours that even part-time work cannot be considered. What then of provision of care for a full day?

## Daycare

Full daycare is virtually non-existent in Northern Ireland. In 1978, the overall picture for under-fives was something like this: 72 per cent were not provided for at all; 15 per cent were in primary school; 3.5 per cent were in nursery school; 7.5 per cent were in playgroups; 1.2 per cent were with childminders; and 0.2 per cent were in day nurseries (Hinds, 1984). Since then the number of day nursery places has increased. Even so, Northern Ireland is the worst area in the United Kingdom and the EC for this type of provision and this thus represents a severe restraint on women working. In 1985, there were a mere 384 day nursery places in Northern

Ireland - all of them in the private or voluntary sectors - giving a provision of 2.8 places per 1000 children aged birth-four. The comparable figure for the rest of the United Kingdom that year was 16.7 places per 1000 (Cohen, 1988).

Again, the latest figures show some improvement from this very low base; in 1988, the number of day nursery places was 529, raising the rate to 3.8 per 1000 (DHSS, 1990). All the 19 premises providing day nursery places remain entirely in the private and community sectors; unlike the rest of the EC and United Kingdom, there are no day nurseries provided by local authorities or Government Departments in Northern Ireland. We are reaping the fruits of the 1978 DHSS/DENI Review, which, in the case of full daycare nurseries, attached a very low priority to this form of provision. It is just such provision which is needed to allow mothers to work and to avoid stigmatising groups such as one-parent families (See next Section for further dicussion of this).

Such full daycare provided by local authorities was advocated in submissions to the Review Group, but the Group did:

> not believe that the large scale development of statutory day nurseries would necessarily be the best way forward, and would certainly not be the quickest. (DHSS/DENI, 1978 p 18)

The Departments recognised the acute shortage of statutory full daycare services but preferred what they called "a more flexible and cost effective approach" (*ibid*).

*Childminders*

The demand and need for full daycare has been increasing. There are currently 245,850 women employed and 6,840 women self-employed in Northern Ireland (PPRU, 1989). Around 93,600 mothers, 40 per cent of all mothers, are working; 29,553 of these have children under five and 26,289 have children aged between five and ten years (Cohen, 1988). The large increase in places provided by registered childminders suggests they have been meeting much of the demand. Between 1975 and 1985, registered childminding places increased by 5,587. In 1975, the 274 childminders offered 804 places; by 1985 their number had grown to 2,575, providing 6,391 places (Cohen, 1988); by 1988 the number of minders had risen to 2,872, providing 7,665 places, the equivalent of 56 places per 1,000 children aged 0-4 (DHSS, 1990). Private sector childminding has played a valuable role; often the childminder is the only real option for those who need full daycare for their children.  However, the problems connected with private childminding must also be addressed.  Good childcare provision deserves proper financing.  It is often difficult in a private childminding system to provide proper wages to the minder at a cost which is not prohibitive to the parent.  In a system where individual childminders use their own homes to look after children, it is also difficult to give time or attention to training.  In addition, there is the question of the space and facilities that can be provided in a private home as compared with a day nursery or playgroup.

*After-School Provision*

Very little after-school and holiday care exists in Northern Ireland.  There are part-time summer schemes in many leisure and community centres, and voluntary groups also run a number of summer schemes.  They tend to cater for children aged eight and upwards and to run for between four and six weeks.  They do not assume *"in loco parentis"* care.  The voluntary sector is somewhat better at providing for five-ten year olds than the statutory sector.  Save the Children Fund is the biggest provider for this age group for after-school activities.

There are more than 152,000 children aged five-ten in Northern Ireland, ten per cent of the total population.  Such after-school projects and holiday schemes as do exist come nowhere near catering for this number of children.  To have an option of care for five-ten year olds is not just necessary for children "at risk" or latch-key kids.  Organised, developmental play is necessary for the children of all parents.

**Conflicts of Policy**

In both the United Kingdom and the Republic of Ireland, daycare provision has had a "mainly interventionist function for disturbed, or socially disadvantaged children" (Phillips and Moss, 1988, p 15).  Inadequate though childcare in other EC Member States may be, demand and provision increased substantially when daycare became less stigmatised and more universal.  It is no coincidence that the countries with the worst childcare record also have the lowest levels of employment for women with children.  The *Moss Report* in 1988 illustrated how two related changes occurred in several different countries:  rapid expansion in childcare provision and a change in policy towards seeing childcare as a service for working parents generally.

In France, the first charitable nursery served working mothers; it aimed to increase the workforce and to abolish poverty by facilitating employment for women. Italy moved from catering for "abandoned or needy mothers and for children from very poor families" to catering for employment. When this happened, nursery provision doubled in seven years. The first nursery in Belgium was for children of employed working-class women and publicly-funded nurseries were exclusively for working mothers from low income families. A change in funding arrangements in 1970 opened nurseries to all, and numbers increased from 78, catering for 7,260 children, to 367 catering for 31,000 children in 1985. In Denmark, the first nurseries were for low income families for social need reasons rather than to promote women's employment. Public funding was extended, the concept of preventive services disappeared, so that Denmark, as we have seen, now has by far the best childcare provision in the EC.

In addition, several countries are actively tackling the problem of an integrated approach to children's education, health, development and care. This issue has also concerned those active in childcare in Northern Ireland. For too long, education and childcare have been approached separately by the statutory sector in particular, but also by the voluntary sector. Cohen (1988) noted that poor coordination of services is a problem throughout the United Kingdom, but Northern Ireland lacks the coordinating mechanism which is provided elsewhere in the United Kingdom by the Inter-Departmental Consultative Group on Daycare Services for Under-Fives. Although a similar mechanism was recommended for Northern Ireland in 1978, it has never been established (Cohen, 1988). Moreover, for too long in Northern Ireland the education and development of children has been seen as being in competition with development and opportunities for women.

At the time of the 1978 review of childcare by the joint Department of Health and Social Services/Department of Education group, a separate examination was being conducted by the Children and Young Persons' Review Group, chaired by Sir Harold Black. This review had a strong health and social services base and the care and custody of children was uppermost in people's minds. The thinking of the Black Group prevailed and any possibility of a more open, universal, non-stigmatised policy on childcare was swamped by a combination of financial considerations and concern for care and custody policies. These policies continue to prevail today.

In the mid 1980s, the Minister responsible for Health and Social Services in Northern Ireland demanded a strategic plan for his Department, including plans from each of the four Health and Social Services Boards including policy and plans for childcare services within a framework outlined by the Department. The DHSS prepared *Strategic Planning Guidelines for Health and Social Services Boards* (DHSS, 1986).

As a result, in their strategic plans, the four Health and Social Services Boards emphasised the role of childcare services in supporting "at risk" children and families. The WHSSB acknowledged the influences on its policy of legislative changes, population trends, changing social conditions, economic problems and changes in public and professional attitudes. It considered that its task was to carry out a radical reappraisal of its network of services for children and families and to identify emerging pressures for change and development. In developing the outline policy of DHSSNI into a more detailed strategy, it placed strong emphasis on the preventive aspects of childcare services, and on the development and strengthening of family support and fostering services (WHSSB, 1986 p 91). The Board stated that:

> The primary aim of childcare policy is to assist the family to deal with the social, emotional and intellectual needs of its children through childhood and adolescence. However, the family may need support and must be able to look for this to the wider community in order to prevent the need for children to come into care or remain in care. Where this is not possible, the care provided must allow every opportunity for the normal development of the child's personality, character and abilities in a stable and secure environment. (WHSSB, 1986 p 90)

The Board declared that it would continue to support playgroups; to increase the number of registered childminders (seen as playing an important role in relieving stress within the family); to develop limited paid childminding for children "at risk"; and to draw up guidelines for the registration of private nurseries, of which there were then five in the Board's area. The WHSSB also indicated that it did not propose to provide day nursery facilities in the five-year period to 1992, but expected to offer daycare to children and their parents in existing residential facilities. It stated that it would:

> continue to give priority to children whose needs are greatest
> in the field of daycare services. Attention will focus on those
> children who have been abused, or are in danger of abuse,
> children in areas of social deprivation, children of single parents
> and children with physical or mental handicaps. (WHSSB, 1986
> p 96)

The NHSSB considered a wide range of factors in determining its strategic plan, including poulation trends, marital breakdown, unemployment, low wages, socially deprived parts of its area, child abuse, proposed legislative changes in childcare, social security, health, housing, environment and the political situation in Northern Ireland. The Board concluded:

> In considering the implications of these assumptions, the Board
> became acutely aware that responsibility for assisting families
> to meet the social, emotional and intellectual needs of their
> children through childhood and adolescence cannot and should
> not be seen to rest with Social Services alone. Each profession
> and agency whose role impacts on children, his [sic] carers or
> on the environment in which he lives, must play its part. What
> is lacking is a comprehensive and integrated policy linking
> economic, environmental, housing, health, education and so-
> cial welfare activities. (NHSSB, 1986 p 37)

The strategic plan continued:

> In the light of these factors, the Board believes that in spite of
> a relatively static child population, social and economic trends,
> new legislation and continuing public concern for the protec-
> tion of vulnerable children will lead to increasing demands
> being made on the Board to provide a wider range of services
> with a higher degree of quality assurance, particularly in re-
> spect of children at risk. (*ibid*)

The EHSSB decided that the interpretation and implementation of the broad outline policy set out in the DHSS strategic planning guidelines should take place within the context of the legal remit of the Children and Young Person's Act (NI) 1968, the Matrimonial Causes (NI) Order 1979 and the Domestic Proceedings (NI) Order 1980.

It went on to say that:

> this legislation places certain duties on the Board, the main
> ones being to diminish the need to receive children into care
> or keep them in care or to bring them before a court and to
> protect and care for children in specific circumstances. (EHSSB,
> 1990 p 36)

The EHSSB stated that the upbringing of children is one of the most
important tasks in society and that parents and children should have access
to a range of services to assist children to develop to their full potential.

> However, given the present financial situation, the Board must
> target its services on those children who are at risk of neglect,
> abuse or exploitation and those in greatest need because of
> family circumstances or relationship difficulties. (EHSSB, 1990
> p 53)

The SHSSB plan followed the pattern of the others when it commented:

> The protection of children remains the paramount objective of
> this programme of care.  Further development of the foster
> care programme, particularly for children who are difficult to
> place, is also a priority, since it should lead to a reduced
> dependence on residential care.  Any resources released from
> a reduction in residential places will be redeployed to child
> protection and family support schemes. (SHSSB, 1990 p 55)

It is clear from these quotations that childcare policy in the Health
and Social Services field in Northern Ireland, where the main providers for
young children are based, is narrowly focused, stigmatised and is defi-
nitely not viewed as an aid to working mothers.  In fact, whereas the
policy in the rest of Europe is to open up childcare to all children, in
Northern Ireland it is becoming even more restricted and policy is increasingly being determined by financial considerations.  There is concern that
provision may actually worsen, especially in the largest area, that covered
by the EHSSB.  That Board completed a review of all playgroups with the
aim of rededicating itself to, and reinforcing, the "at risk" principle by
targetting its funding on individual children.  It is moving from funding
playgroups in general towards identifying its funds with particular children

in a playgroup. The Board intended voluntary agencies to seek funds on the basis of their proportion of "at risk" children (EHSSB, 1987). The Board's review of services for under-fives showed that voluntary agencies were catering for "at risk" children, but in a non-threatening, non-stigmatised environment at a playgroup open to all. One major childcare agency whose proportion of "at risk" children is considerably lower than that in the Board's own provision, nonetheless covers more such children than the Board does. This provision, however, may be forced to change in the light of statutory policy and funding.

Playgroups struggle for funds and 60 per cent of groups in the Eastern area have to operate without any public funding. It has been highlighted both at United Kingdom and at EC level that Northern Ireland playgroup workers rely on low wages and temporary employment schemes. There is widespread acceptance that this has a detrimental effect on the quality of care (Cohen, 1988; Moss, 1988).

Voluntary childcare agencies have insisted that the base criteria proposed by the Board should be widened by taking the two categories "at risk" and "in need" together. "At risk" is defined to mean that the child's most crucial needs - safety, nutrition, emotional security, opportunity to learn - are not being met to the extent that s/he requires protection and/ or compensatory experience. "In need" means that the child's personal or family circumstances diminish her or his opportunity for normal childhood development and there is a failure or partial failure to meet his or her needs - for emotional security, opportunity to learn, opportunity to play and relate to others - to the extent that she or he requires parental care to be supplemented by compensatory experience. It is clear, however, that the focus of childcare is narrowing and that fewer and fewer children will be able to obtain publicly-funded places in playgroups. One example of this is the removal of the access of many lone parents to the provision. Previously all lone parents could be considered for places since their children were all considered to be "at risk" or "in need". Lone parents will not in future benefit from public funding for playgroup places unless they are deemed to require "special" support. The EHSSB states:

> whilst there might be some disappointment that such a strategy
> does not aim to provide services for young children as of right,
> the present legislative remit and resources available make it
> impossible for the Board to adopt such an approach. Given
> these constraints, the Board must discriminate in favour of the
> children most at risk or in need. (EHSSB, 1987 p 27)

# CONCLUSION

Both a comparative examination of childcare provision and a detailed consideration of statutory policy and practice locally show that childcare in Northern Ireland has little to do with planning or vision and much to do with antiquated atttitudes and economic pressures.  Elsewhere in the United Kingdom, policy is beginning to change under pressure from the demographic decline which will make women essential to the labour force over the next decade.  So, while Ministers increasingly talk about the need to expand childcare, Government Departments and other agencies pursue different, often conflicting, policies.

A telling example lies in the 1990 Budget announcement that some childcare provision provided by employers will no longer be taxed, a change which should, in principle, encourage female workers to return to work.  Publication of the Finance Bill, however, revealed this to be a concession hedged round with restrictions, among them that the childcare must be provided on premises made available by the employer alone, or under arrangements where the employer is still wholly or partly responsible for financing **and** managing the provision of care.  DENI sought in March 1990 (the month of the Budget) to persuade schools to make spare rooms available for childcare purposes.  It said:

> It is considered that employers will increasingly come to see economic and practical advantage in providing childcare facilities for their employees through schemes based in school premises rather than through setting up schemes of their own, and agree to assist, directly or indirectly, with their funding. (DENI, 1990b p 32)

While a policy to open up schools in this way is to be welcomed, at the time of writing it was at variance with the Finance Bill because such childcare would still be taxable if the employer were involved in funding, but not managing, the childcare provision.  Indeed, the scope of the Finance Bill could prove to be very limited indeed since only three per cent of employers provide workplace nurseries (Hansard, 12.2.1990, Col 77).  It is worth noting that even the Northern Ireland Civil Service (NICS), the largest employer in Northern Ireland, does not provide day nurseries for its staff.  Indeed, there are no workplace nurseries in Northern Ireland currently.  The Finance Bill, therefore, will provide no benefits for children or working parents in Northern Ireland unless employers and trade unions address their responsibilities to set up workplace nurseries. Even more serious is that thinking in Northern Ireland appears to have gone into reverse, putting more emphasis than before on restricting childcare to a small minority of children "at risk" or "in need" instead of opening it to all who want it for their children, as is the more normal pattern throughout the EC. Certainly the policy statements from DHSS and Boards betray no awareness of the need to begin to provide a universal service or to make it easier for women to work.

It is understandable that Health and Social Services Boards and Education and Library Boards interpret their roles and priorities within the legal framework and policy created by Government. Since there is no statutory duty to provide nursery education, they have not seen it as important to do so; since there are duties to look after children "at risk" and "in need", these are seen as priorities. However, this narrow focus makes it virtually impossible to respond to important changes in society and the labour market. Childcare for working mothers cannot be provided through a policy which concentrates on a minority of disadvantaged children. And while particular attention should be paid to special need children, this can be done in a far better manner. It is not conducive to children's development to label or stigmatise them, or for them (or their parents) to feel that their parents have been labelled "inadequate" or "unable to cope". All children should have equal access to opportunities for development, education and enrichment without having to be singled out.

Against the trend across the rest of the EC, Northern Ireland is witnessing the narrowing of childcare services and the stigmatising of women and their families, with what little childcare policy and provision there is retreating into the negative framework of failure and compensation. Childcare policy should be about growth and development for all children and about providing mothers and fathers with the flexibility and support they need. Proper childcare is not something which is gained for working women at the expense of children; it is a provision for the benefit of women and children.

This is particularly important in the context of equal opportunities for women. Government policies have restricted the ability of women to take their place in the labour market. The lack of career breaks, for example, tends to force women back into the traditional role of mother and housekeeper, and even now, when female labour is needed, the Government is unwilling to commit public funds to childminding services. The provision that does exist is largely unsuitable for working mothers; the hours of nursery schools and playgroups, for example, would permit part-time work at most. Mothers working full-time have to find a place in one of the rare day nurseries or to use childminders. They have to set up arrangements to ferry children from school to childminder and back home again. School holidays can be a nightmare and a financial drain if care is required throughout the day. All these factors put women at a distinct disadvantage in competing for employment. As Moss has said:

> The essential point to be restated and emphasised is that the conditions under which men and women supply their labour to the labour market are not equal; and that this inequality is neither inherent nor inevitable but is socially determined...as a consequence, wage rates and occupational position are not determined purely by market forces but the social costs of reproduction which are unequally distributed. (Moss, 1988 p 36)

Proper facilities, good wages and training cost money. Good quality childcare is not cheap, and the cost is prohibitive for those on average and low incomes. Northern Ireland's childcare largely depends on (female) childminders who, in turn, are badly paid and receive little training or support. While some daycare services could be assisted with resources from employers and voluntary organisations, childcare must be recognised adequately in the public purse through statutory provision, public funding of community-based schemes, complete tax concessions for daycare nurseries no matter who funds or manages them, and subsidies for parents. In addition, there should be greater recognition in the benefit system of the childcare costs of lone parents. Above all, a comprehensive policy on childcare for all children is needed rather than the patchy, *ad hoc* method of operating at present. There should be a lead Department responsible for this policy, but Health and Social Services, Education and Economic Development, at least, should be involved.

What needs to be recognised in what has been essentially a debate to date about childcare responsibility in terms of education and health, is the place of economic development. With such a more open approach to childcare, opportunities could be created and seized to assist with funding the necessary provision. Bringing economic factors into the equation opens up possibilities such as the use of EC Structural Funds to provide childcare services:

Financial support for the development of childcare services can assist in meeting Structural Funding objectives through:

- establishing infrastructures essential in maximising and developing local skill resources in areas which are less developed or affected by industrial decline

- facilitating women's access to education and training

- assisting women's integration into employment and the desegregation of the labour market and offsetting current and projected skill shortages in all countries

- stimulating rural development and the diversification of the rural economy through facilitating a greater and substantial economic role for women within rural areas.
(Cohen, 1989 p 1)

Cohen draws attention to the fact that Community Support Frameworks for the implementation of the European Regional Development Plans prepared in each Member State of the EC will now include a standard clause drawing attention to the existence of, and the need to take account of, equality legislation and policy. This clause will highlight the necessity of giving consideration to training and infrastructure requirements which facilitate labour force participation by women with children. She argues that this clause could be used actively to secure funding for childcare provision.

A useful recommendation in the Select Committee Report on educational provision for the under-fives is that the Departments of Health and Education and Science in Great Britain should establish a thorough survey of the existing demand for the various forms of provision for the under-fives. It suggests that this should be done along with the Department of Employment because of the labour market effects. Similar research could usefully be carried out by the different agencies involved in Northern Ireland.

Probably the best chance at present of changing thinking and improving provision in the United Kingdom is within the context of the European Community. For Northern Ireland women in particular, it is crucially important that the recommendations of the *Moss Report* are pursued. The most important of these are an EC Framework Directive on childcare services and a Directive to guarantee entitlement to maternity leave, parental leave and leave for family reasons. A further three recommendations include an EC-funded European programme on childcare and equality of opportunity, a guide to good practice for fathers' participation in family responsibility, and assistance to Member States with low levels of national income to develop childcare services for employed parents. Policies such as these would be important steps in halting Northern Ireland's policy reversals on childcare as described in this Chapter.

# REFERENCES

BRADSHAW J., (1989) *Social Security Parity in Northern Ireland*, Occasional Paper, Belfast: Policy Research Institute

COHEN B., (1988) *Caring for Children: Services and Policies for Childcare and Equal Opportunities in the United Kingdom - Report of the European Commission's Childcare Network*, London: Commission of the European Communities

COHEN B., (1989) *Structural Funding and Childcare: Current Funding Applications and Policy Implications*, Brussels: Commission of the European Communities, Directorate General Employment, Industrial Relations and Social Affairs

DEPARTMENT OF EDUCATION FOR NORTHERN IRELAND, (1988) "Pupils and Teachers in Grant-Aided Schools", DENI Statistical Bulletin

DEPARTMENT OF EDUCATION FOR NORTHERN IRELAND, (1990a) *Education Reform: What It Means to You*, Belfast: DENI

DEPARTMENT OF EDUCATION FOR NORTHERN IRELAND, (1990b) "The Use of School Premises for Childcare Provision out of School Hours", DENI Circular 1990/5

DEPARTMENT OF HEALTH AND SOCIAL SERVICES, (1986) "Strategic Planning Guidelines for Health and Personal Social Services", DHSS Circular HSS[P] 1/86

DEPARTMENT OF HEALTH AND SOCIAL SERVICES, (1990) DHSS Policy statement submitted to EOCNI Childcare Working Group

DEPARTMENT OF HEALTH AND SOCIAL SERVICES/DEPARTMENT OF EDUCATION FOR NORTHERN IRELAND, (1978) *Daycare and Education for the Under-Fives in Northern Ireland: Policy and Objectives*, Belfast: DHSS/DENI

EASTERN HEALTH AND SOCIAL SERVICES BOARD, (1986) *Area Strategic Plan 1987-1992*, Belfast: EHSSB

EASTERN HEALTH AND SOCIAL SERVICES BOARD, (1987) "Social Services Department Review of Services for Under-Fives within the Eastern Health and Social Services Board" (unpublished paper)

EASTERN HEALTH AND SOCIAL SERVICES BOARD, (1990) *EHSSB Operational Plan 1990-91*, Belfast:  EHSSB

EMPLOYMENT GAZETTE, (1989) "Labour Force Outlook to the Year 2000", April, Belfast:  DED

*GUARDIAN*, 18 January 1989

HINDS B., (1984) *So You Want to Start a Day Nursery?  Here's How*, Belfast: Gingerbread (NI)

HINDS B., (1985) *Who Cares? Reviewing Today's Provision in Changing Patterns of Family and Childcare Needs in Northern Ireland*, Conference report, Belfast: National Council for Voluntary Childcare Organisations (NI)

INDUSTRIAL DEVELOPMENT BOARD FOR NORTHERN IRELAND, (1989) *Widening Horizons: A Perspective on the Skill Shortages of the 90s*, Belfast: IDBNI

JOSHI H., (1987) "The Cost of Caring", in C. Glendinning and J. Millar (Eds), *Women and Poverty in Britain*, Brighton: Wheatsheaf

McSHANE L., (1987) "Day nurseries in Northern Ireland 1941-1955: Gender Ideology in Social Policy", in P. Jackson and B. O'Connor (Eds), *Gender in Irish Society*, Galway:  Galway University Press

MAGUIRE M, and WARD P., (1989) *A Case Study of Labour Turnover in a Northern Ireland Clothing Company*, Belfast:  PRI

MARTIN J. and ROBERTS C., (1984) *Women and Employment:  A Lifetime Perspective*, London:  HMSO

MOSS P., (1988) *Childcare and Equality of Opportunity - Consolidated Report to the European Commission*, Brussels: Commission of the European Communities, Directorate General Employment, Social Affairs and Education

NORTHERN HEALTH AND SOCIAL SERVICES BOARD, (1986) *Area Strategic Plan 1987-1992*, Ballymena:  NHSSB

NORTHERN IRELAND TRAINING AUTHORITY, (1988) *The Provision and Acquisition of Key Skills in the Northern Ireland Clothing Industry*, Newtownabbey, Co Antrim:  NITA

PHILLIPS A. and MOSS P., (1988) *Who Cares for Europe's Children - The Short Report of the European Childcare Network*, Brussels: Commission of the European Communities, Directorate General Employment, Social Affairs and Education

POLICY, PLANNING AND RESEARCH UNIT, (1989) *Northern Ireland Annual Abstract of Statistics*, Belfast:  PPRU

SELECT COMMITTEE ON EDUCATION, SCIENCE AND ARTS, (1988) *Educational Provision for the Under-Fives - First Report*, London: HMSO

SOUTHERN HEALTH AND SOCIAL SERVICES BOARD, (1990) *SHSSB Operational Plan 1990-1991*, Portadown:  SHSSB

TRAINING AGENCY, (1990) *Labour Market Quarterly Report*, London: Training Agency, Employment Department

*ULSTER NEWSLETTER*, 2 March 1983

WESTERN HEALTH AND SOCIAL SERVICES BOARD, (1986) *Strategic Plan and Review for the Health and Personal Social Services 1987-1992*, Campsie:  WHSSB

WITHERSPOON S., (1985) "Sex Roles and Gender Issues", in R. Jowell and S. Witherspoon (Eds), *British Social Attitudes: The 1985 Report*, Aldershot: Gower

# CHAPTER SEVEN

# GENDER AND OPPORTUNITY IN THE YOUTH TRAINING PROGRAMME*

## PAMELA MONTGOMERY

## INTRODUCTION

With a budget totalling nearly half of the entire expenditure on training in Northern Ireland, the Youth Training Programme (YTP) reflects government emphasis on youth training within overall training policy. The central aims of the programme are "to lay the foundation of a skilled flexible workforce" and "to help all 16 and 17 year olds make the transition from school to adult working life" (DMS/DENI, 1982). The programme was launched in 1982 and is administered by an Inter-Departmental Executive (IDE) of the Department of Economic Development (DED) and the Department of Education for Northern Ireland (DENI). YTP currently offers all 16 year olds a two-year training programme comprising work experience, skill training and further education and caters for just over one in five of all schoolleavers in Northern Ireland (Duffy and McWhirter, 1987).

Throughout its lifespan, YTP has been characterised by constant modification which has produced changes in the overall structure and functioning of the programme. In broad terms, policy developments since 1982 have paralleled those in the Youth Training Scheme (YTS) in Great Britain, with attempts made to move the programme as far as possible towards an employer-led model of training and to improve the quality of training. However, in contrast to YTS, where a history of policy development on the issue of equal opportunities for girls can be traced from the outset, the question of equal opportunities has not been an explicit issue in YTP. From its publicity which commonly presents images of girls and boys and its policy statements which resolutely refer to training opportunities for young people one might assume that equal opportunity for girls

117

and boys is an intended goal of YTP. There is no doubt that on paper at least, YTP offers considerable potential for meeting this goal. Against this, Whyte et al's (1985) study of day-to-day practice, while not focusing on equal opportunity issues, expressed doubts as to whether girls were "getting a fair deal" (*ibid* p 161, cf Rees, 1983).

Drawing on the findings of a project which focused specifically on equal opportunities in YTP (Montgomery and Davies, 1990) this Chapter will explore why a training programme, which on the face of it ought to provide girls with the opportunity to avail themselves of the full range of training options and participate fully in all sections of the labour market, in practice replicates and reinforces existing gender divisions in the labour market.

The Chapter begins by exploring the specific context in which youth training measures emerged and speculates as to why, given the prominence of the issue in YTS in Great Britain and the various criticisms which emerged in the early days of the operation of the programme, equal opportunities for girls has, until recently, failed to be addressed in Northern Ireland in YTP at policy level. The Chapter then provides a brief outline of the organisation and structure of training under YTP and highlights those particular aspects of the programme which, in principle, ought to compensate for disadvantage and encourage equality of opportunity. It will be shown that this potential has not been realised and that training remains highly segregated by gender. Drawing on interviews with scheme managers, staff and trainees, the Chapter will try to account for gender segregation in training and, focusing on the experience of girls who have attempted to obtain training in non-traditional areas, will highlight some of the processes by which girls are denied access and confined to training courses which offer entry into jobs which conform to traditional notions of "women's work". The final Section draws on policy developments in YTS in Great Britain and explores some of the policy options available for developing real equality of opportunity in YTP.

### Context of Youth Training Measures

With its forerunner the Youth Opportunities Programme (YOP), YTP emerged in the context of grave concern regarding spiraling levels of youth unemployment. Throughout the 1970s, the continued effects of the economic recession, young people's position in the secondary labour market, and the increasing numbers of young people entering the labour market had combined to produce a disproportionate effect on employment opportunities for the

under 20s in Northern Ireland and in the United Kingdom as a whole
(Cockburn, 1987; Finn, 1987; Buswell, 1988). The situation was exacer-
bated by the increasing availability of a pool of unemployed adult workers
which Finn has argued were preferred by employers who perceived young
workers as irresponsible, and unmotivated for work. It was in this context
that YOP was established in Northern Ireland in 1977 and one year later
in Great Britain.

Maguire and Roper (1990) have argued that YOP was in essence a
reactive scheme primarily set up to deal with large numbers of unemployed young people. Not surprisingly, YOP schemes in both Great Britain
and Northern Ireland soon ran into difficulties and were quickly undermined in the face of a general lack of confidence and public criticism. In
addition to accusations of poor training, exploitation of young workers and
substitution of permanent employees by trainees, a major problem was the
credibility gap between the representation of the scheme as a route to
permanent employment and the ever growing numbers of unemployed
young people.

In the face of growing disenchantment with YOP, a general lack of
confidence in existing training structures to meet the needs of a changing
economy and the emergence of a broad ideology of "new vocationalism"
in education and training, the Manpower Services Commission (MSC) in
Great Britain published *The New Training Initiative* in 1981. This set the
goal of:

> moving towards a position where all young people under the
> age of 18 have the opportunity of either continuing full-time
> education or entering training or a period of planned work
> experience combining work-related training and education; (MSC,
> 1981 p 4)

and paved the way for the YTS in Great Britain. By January 1982, a new
policy document was available in Northern Ireland outlining proposals for
a new youth training programme. YTP was launched in September of that
year, one full year before YTS in Great Britain.

Unlike YOP, which was largely an unemployment measure, YTP
emerged in the wider context of a plan to restructure training for both
adults and young people within which the focus was placed squarely on
skill training. Rees and Rees (1982) have argued that state intervention
in periods of high youth unemployment has been underpinned by a concern about the detrimental effects of unemployment on young people and

the potential threat of social and civil disorder. Analysing debates about youth unemployment, Rees (1983, 1984) has argued that this concern is, in fact, concern about the possible threat posed by unemployed young men rather than unemployed young women:

> Time and time again, in the 1930's as well as the 1970s and 1980s, the "opinion forming elite" identify unemployed young men as being the threat to [sic] disorder. It is they who will it is feared, start the revolution, become vandals and criminals, join extremist groups, start riots and so on. The adverse effects on girls are scarcely mentioned except in terms of promiscuity or prostitution. (Rees, 1984 p 5)

In a study of opportunities for girls and boys in YOP in Northern Ireland, Rees (1983) found that not only were girls concentrated in the cheaper schemes and schemes for the less able, many were training for occupations which were at that time in serious decline. She interpreted her findings as indicative of a lack of concern about female youth unemployment in Northern Ireland and argued that in the context of real civil and political unrest, the focus was on unemployed young men who were perceived as being at risk of being drawn into paramilitary organisations. Within such a framework, female unemployment does not represent a problem since it is assumed that young women do not get involved in "the Troubles" and as such no special provision is required.

Whatever the reason for it, there is no evidence that equal opportunities for girls was an explicit issue in YOP. Writing just before the introduction of YTP, Rees (1983) predicted that the gender segregation and ghettoisation of girls in training for traditional "women's work" would be repeated in the new youth training measures. While not focusing directly on gender issues, Whyte et al's (1985) study of YTP in its second year of operation, suggested that this was being borne out. They drew attention to the serious underrepresentation of girls in some of the schemes, particularly those provided by Training Centres, which offer training in traditional craft skills, and Community Workshops, which offer training in a broader range of skills, and to the fact that relative to boys, fewer girls found employment on leaving YTP. In their conclusion to the report, the authors raised a series of questions about the programme's treatment of girls:

> One might ask whether the Government Training Centres and
> Community Workshops are directing sufficient publicity about
> their courses towards girls. Why are girls so reluctant to apply
> to these training schemes? Are employment opportunities for
> girls more limited even if they do acquire these skills? Is the
> inhibition a cultural phenomenon...We must ask therefore whether
> girls on the Youth Training Programme are getting a fair deal
> and why they are not having as much success as boys in find-
> ing employment. Are they not being exposed to the same
> extent as boys during training to skills which would be useful
> in the labour market? Are they not oriented sufficiently in
> their own minds to the realities of the demands of employ-
> ment? Is the programme not geared to meet their needs at
> present? (Whyte et al, 1985 p 161-162)

Despite these misgivings, it was not until 1988, five years after the publication
of Rees' findings and three years after Whyte et al's study that the issue
of equality of opportunity for girls was finally raised within YTP. Work
began in that year in planning three single sex schemes for girls in non-
traditional training areas and in drafting an Equal Opportunities Code.
The planned single sex schemes appear to have run into difficulties and
in the event, none of these schemes actually ran. The Code, in preparation
for nearly two years, has yet to be published. One must conclude that
while equality of opportunity is now on the policy agenda of IDE, the
issue has far from priority status. In many ways YTP offers real potential
for providing girls with a route out of the dead-end jobs which are a
feature of many women's lives today. The next Section provides a brief
outline of how training was structured at the point at which fieldwork for
the project was carried out in 1989 and highlights those particular aspects
of the programme which in theory, at least, ought to facilitate equality of
opportunity (See Montgomery and Davies, 1990).

## Organisation and Structure of Training in YTP

YTP is a highly complex programme. This is reflected in the range of
different providers delivering training, the varying courses and schemes on
offer, differences in provision in scheme types in first and second year
training and the joint administration of the programme which produces
dispersion between government departments of information and statistics
relevant to the programme. In general terms, YTP offers minimum-age
schoolleavers two years of provision with training designed around three

elements:  work experience, skill-training and further education.  In effect, this has always amounted to two separate one-year units rather than a fully integrated two-year programme.  First year provision is required to provide broad-based training with courses intended to cross occupational boundaries in keeping with the broad aim of YTP as the foundation of a skilled, flexible workforce.  Further education is normally provided by a local Further Education College, with skill training provided by the scheme and work experience either provided by the scheme or by local employers.  Second year provision is required to provide young people with the opportunity for specialisation in one skill.

There are four main providers of training under YTP:  12 Training Centres which also provide adult training, 44 Community Workshops, 26 Further Education Colleges which also provide a range of further education courses for adults, and employers.  While Training Centres provide training largely in the fields of engineering and construction, Community Workshops, Further Education Colleges and employers offer a wider range of training.  First year provision is divided more or less equally between these four providers.  The bulk of second year training is provided by employers under Workscheme within which young people have employee status and receive employment and training.  A smaller number of trainee places is available for 17 year olds, concentrated in Community Workshops, with additional places provided by Further Education Colleges, Youth and Community Projects and the Young Help Trust.  Table 7.1 gives a summary of overall provision for the year 1988.

There is a considerable volume of recent research in Great Britain to suggest that the life and school experience of girls will commonly have limited their occupational expectations and aspirations (Jenkins, 1983; Griffin, 1985; Furlong, 1986; Coffield et al, 1986; Cockburn, 1987; Holland, 1988), and YTP, on paper, has a number of features that would serve to combat this.  First, in principle, all training places are open to all young people regardless of previous experience, of subject choice at school, and of academic achievement or qualifications.  In this way, the programme potentially offers the opportunity of counteracting the school and life experiences of girls, many of whom will have failed or been failed by the school system and who have low aspirations, expectations and confidence.  Second, career guidance and advice is built into the programme, with access to the majority of training places through the Careers Service and additional information on training opportunities supplied by individual schemes in a pre-training interview before the young people actually take up their places.  This guidance could play a vital role in making girls

Table 7.1:  YTP: Total Number of Providers and Places, 1988

|  | No. of Providers | Places Available | |
|---|---|---|---|
|  |  | First Year | Second Year |
| Training Centres | 12 | 1,631 | 150 |
| Employer-Led Schemes (approx) | 50 | 1,860 | ** |
| Community Workshops | 44 | 2,120 | 1,690 |
| Colleges of Further Education | 26 | 1,965 | 573 |
| Youth Community Projects | 13 | ** | 230 |
| Young Help | 7 | ** | 337 |
| Workscheme | na | ** | 6,000 |
| Recognised Training Organisations | 6 | 455 | 265 |
| Totals |  | 8,031 | 9,245 |

Key:  na = not available,  ** = not applicable

Source:  Montgomery and Davies, 1990

aware of the full range of training options available, none of which require prior qualifications or experience. Third, the structure of training in the first year, with its broad-based emphasis, potentially offers the opportunity of challenging the impact of the gender segregation and sex-typing in activities many girls will have experienced in school, so that the possibility is open for girls to sample a range of training options, including those in non-traditional areas. Finally, the mode of assessment employed in YTP, the City and Guilds Profiling System, with its emphasis on personal development and consultation between trainer and trainee, could provide the framework for development of the self-worth and confidence of girls and hence raise their sights and aspirations.

Despite these features, which together suggest a training programme which ought to deliver equal opportunities to girls and boys, available statistics point to the view that this potential for achieving equality of opportunity has not been realised. This is documented in the next Section.

## Girls and Boys in YTP

Department of Economic Development (DED) statistics on the numbers of girls and boys entering YTP since 1984 show that boys have consistently outnumbered girls, with the current ratio of boys to girls around 2:1 (Montgomery and Davies, 1990). The YTP Cohort study, a longitudinal investigation of the post-16 routes followed by a sample of 1,890 young people eligible to leave school in 1984, suggests that differences in this overall rate of participation can be accounted for by the higher proportion of girls remaining in full-time education after school leaving age while boys are more evenly divided between full-time education and YTP (McWhirter, nd). It is difficult to assess the precise impact of this 2:1 imbalance on girls' prospects in the labour market as it is not possible to say with any certainty which of the three main post-16 routes, remaining at school, finding employment, or entering YTP, is the most advantageous as far as life chances are concerned (See Montgomery and Davies, 1990). In this context, it is more appropriate to focus on how girls and boys are distributed throughout YTP and on what kinds of training they are actually receiving.

The DED routinely collects statistics on the proportion of girls and boys in different kinds of provision. From these statistics it is clear that the proportion of girls and boys in training varies considerably by provider type.

Table 7.2:   Sex of Trainees in Full-Time Training Schemes
by Provider (30.9.1988)

| Provider | Numbers in Training | Percent Male | Female |
|---|---|---|---|
| Community Workshops | 3,332 | 69 | 32 |
| Further Education Colleges | 2,003 | 55 | 45 |
| Employer-Led | 1,951 | 45 | 55 |
| Training Centres | 1,839 | 100 | 0 |
| Young Help | 238 | 12 | 88 |
| Youth Community Project | 169 | 65 | 36 |
| Total | 9,532 | 66 | 34 |

Source:  Montgomery and Davies, 1990

Girls are almost totally excluded from that sector of the labour market represented by the vocational courses on offer in Training Centres. Among over 1,800 trainees receiving training in Training Centres in September 1988, only one was female. Girls are concentrated in Further Education Colleges and Employer Schemes with only the Community Workshops approaching the overall 2:1 average. Interesting as these provider statistics are, they say little about the specific type of training girls are actually receiving. Unfortunately the take-up of places on different vocational courses offered by providers is not currently monitored by sex, so that it is not possible to determine from routine statistics what kinds of training girls and boys are receiving under YTP. However, from statistics routinely collected by DENI on the type of further education young people are receiving in Further Education Colleges as part of their course, it is possible to build up a partial picture of the kinds of training in which girls and boys are engaged.

The evidence suggests that training courses provided under YTP are highly segregated by sex. Of 17 classifiable courses offered by Further Education Colleges, only 5 could be described as mixed to any degree (Figure 7.1). Similarly, only 4 of the 25 classifiable courses provided by the colleges to young people in connection with other providers' courses were mixed (Figure 7.2). It can be seen that courses in construction, engineering and electronics which might be expected to lead to clear credentials and career possibilities had only a handful of girls. Courses in caring services, personal services, office practice, travel and tourism, on the other hand, where credentials and prospects are scarcer, had only a handful of boys. These statistics suggest that overwhelmingly, girls were being confined to preparation for women's work.

It is hard to be optimistic about girls' prospects in the labour market given the type of training they are receiving under YTP. Girls are virtually absent from Training Centres and from the kinds of training that generate craft skills and the hope of good prospects and income in the manual sector that these entail; instead they are being trained for employment in areas traditionally open to women and areas traditionally disadvantaged in terms of pay and future prospects.

From what information is available, then, on the kinds of training girls and boys are receiving in YTP, it would appear that the programme has done little to widen girls' horizons. The following Section draws on a study of the day-to-day practice of six schemes providing training under YTP. The study employed a range of techniques including a series of semi-structured interviews with scheme managers and a sample of scheme

Figure 7.1:   Courses Taken by Girls and Boys in Further Education
College Provision (1988-1989)

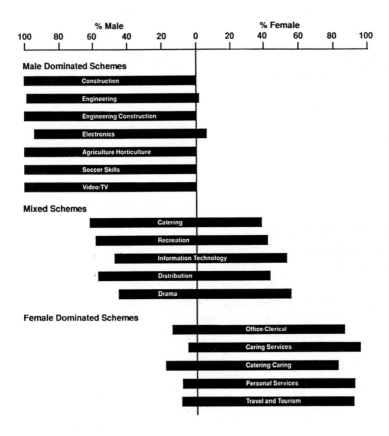

Source:   Montgomery and Davies, 1990

Figure 7.2:  Further Education Courses Taken by Girls and Boys
as Part of Other Provision (October, 1988)

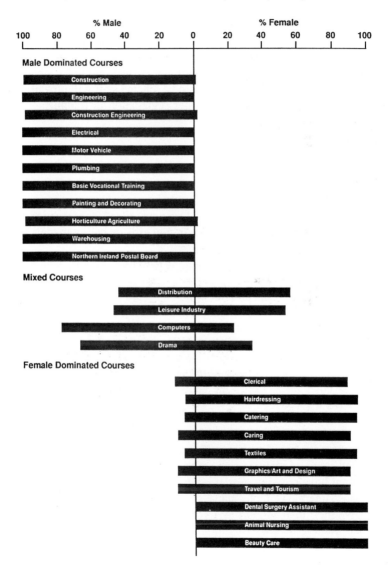

Source:  Montgomery and Davies, 1990

staff (N=2O), semi-structured interviews and group discussions with a sample of trainees (N=88; 43 girls and 45 boys) which were supplemented by information obtained from questionnaires, observation of training procedures and informal discussions with staff and trainees. It will be argued that in the absence of a specific policy development initiative, of strong commitment to an equal opportunities goal and of clear guidance from the top as to how equality of opportunity for girls might be achieved, the beliefs, attitudes and values of grassroots scheme staff will prevail, and will act to maintain and reinforce gender segregation in training.

### Barriers to Non-traditional Training

In the course of interviews with scheme managers and staff, all were asked for their views on gender segregation in training, and how they would see the introduction of specific initiatives in their own schemes to encourage girls and boys to take up non-traditional training. Gender segregation was evident in all of the schemes visited, with few girls or boys pursuing non-traditional training.

While staff were aware that training in their own schemes was highly segregated by sex, this was perceived as a "fact of life" by the majority of scheme staff, rather than an issue which ought to be addressed. Indeed, most felt that the factors underlying gender segregation in YTP were so entrenched that nothing could be done to produce change.

> We don't go out to segregate them...we find girls segregate themselves. We can't change the attitudes of society. All we can do is say, "There's the options, pick what you want".
> (Male Manager)

Attitudes to non-traditional training were more complex and deserve close consideration. In broad terms, staff reactions were of three main types; unqualified support, qualified support and resistance. Unqualified support for girls and boys crossing gender boundaries in training was rare. Only two of those interviewed, one manager and one instructor, stated that they would give their total support to a young person of either sex wishing to undertake training in a non-traditional field.

> The attitude of [the scheme] is if you want a bash, go on and try it. Everyone should have the opportunity to try what they want. (Female Manager)

The qualified support some staff expressed was rooted in two factors; traditional attitudes regarding the relative appropriateness of particular jobs for girls and boys and concern about the future employability of trainees. For a number of staff, the notion of girls crossing gender boundaries was acceptable for certain traditionally male occupations but not for others. In these cases, staff simply expanded the range of "appropriate" female jobs rather than taking on board the concept of all jobs being equally appropriate for both sexes. What was deemed appropriate/inappropriate varied. In general, however, it was the "heavy trades" which were regarded as inappropriate for women. In a number of cases, staff stated that they would warn a trainee that it might be difficult to get a job after completing training, since employers were perceived as being highly traditional and unlikely to employ girls in traditionally male areas of employment. This sometimes even worked in reverse:

> If a boy wants to do hairdressing, I won't say no, but I may point out that it may be difficult to break in to. (Female instructor)

The third response, characterised by direct resistance to non-traditional training, was fairly widespread, with over half of the 20 staff interviewed stating they would not personally be in favour of girls and boys crossing gender boundaries in training and some, indeed, stating quite explicitly that this should be actively discouraged. Again, this response was rooted in and justified by a concern for young people's future employability.

> What employer would employ a girl as a bricklayer? She wouldn't be accepted in the industry. At the end of the day, the most important thing is for the young people to get jobs. (Female Instructor)

Not surprisingly then, when asked whether they would favour initiatives in their own schemes to encourage girls and boys to consider non-traditional training, the majority of staff expressed little support. A further factor at work in their thinking here related to "choice" and the need, as they saw it, to protect trainee choice. Perceiving gender segregation in training as a result of young people's free choice, meant it was a "fact of life" and hence outside the responsibility of staff. In addition, in several of the schemes visited, staff appeared to equate initiatives designed to encourage young people to avail themselves of the full range of training opportunities with "forcing young people to do something they don't want to do". Instead, the "push", they felt, should come from the young people themselves. It seemed to them self-evident that all training places were open to girls and boys, with isolated examples of girls who had crossed gender boundaries in training in their own schemes in the past put forward to substantiate this claim. Overall, therefore, the interviews reveal a framework of thinking about equal opportunities and potential "discrimination" that focuses solely on access to training places and on the presence or absence of explicit regulations excluding girls or boys for particular types of training. Within this conceptual framework, the absence of such regulations is taken as *prima facie* evidence that the programme and individual schemes are providing equal opportunities. Since all training places were perceived as open to all, gender segregation was attributed to young people's free choice which was most often seen as outside the sphere of the programme. This is a concept of equal opportunities which ignores the constraints on girls (and sometimes too on boys), which limit their occupational choice. Within such a framework and in the context of traditional attitudes about which jobs are appropriate for girls and boys and concerns about the future employability of trainees who have undertaken non-traditional training, it seems unlikely that the features of the programme identified earlier as offering potential for providing equality of opportunity, will actually work to widen horizons for girls.

Observations of training and interviews with staff in the six schemes visited provided support for this view. First, while all training places were perceived as open to girls and boys, there was an expectation that girls and boys would want a traditional training place. This was clearly in evidence in the schemes' promotional literature which depicted girls and boys training in traditional areas; girls in hairdressing, in office settings and caring for children or the elderly; boys using machinery and in industrial settings. Second, while all young people were provided with information on training opportunities in each of the individual schemes in the course of an interview which took place before they began training, in none of the schemes were the young people provided with information on the full range of training options. Staff either provided information only on those areas asked about or used informal procedures such as asking about hobbies and then putting forward selected suggestions as to what options the young person might like to consider. Such options are likely to reflect the individual attitudes of the member of staff concerned regarding the appropriateness of particular jobs for girls and boys. Third, while broad-based training and the City and Guilds Profiling system offer potential for encouraging girls to sample the full range of training opportunities available, neither of these features of YTP was designed with an equal opportunities goal in mind. Given the attitudinal climate, it is not surprising that none of the providers appeared to be using job-sampling or profiling to create equality of opportunity.

As it currently functions then, YTP, rather than widening young peoples' horizons, channels them into gender-appropriate training which will prepare them for traditional areas of employment. For girls this means low paid, low status jobs.

The process by which girls are excluded from non-traditional training is most clearly illustrated through the experience of a number of girls interviewed in the course of the study who stated that they had considered non-traditional training in the past and wanted to try such training (N=11). Despite this desire for training in, for example, motor vehicle repair or painting and decorating, all but one of the girls were training for traditionally female jobs at the time of the visit. This is consistent with research conducted in Great Britain which suggests that despite the fact that the majority of girls end up training for traditionally female jobs, a sizeable minority do consider training in non-traditional areas. A recent study by Holland (1988), for example, while documenting sex-stereotyping in girls' occupational aspirations, found that as many as 41 per cent aspired to employment in traditionally male areas. More importantly perhaps, when asked whether they expected to achieve their ambition, only 19 per cent felt they would. From the interviews, it would appear that by the time they reach YTP, some girls will have given up hope and settled for the safe option of gender congruent training. The role of school experience was mentioned as a contributing factor in this decision by a number of girls who stated that they had never had the chance to study relevant "boys" subjects at school and were unsure about what they would be letting themselves in for, were they to change direction.

There was evidence too that the careers advice girls receive may discourage non-traditional training, as may parental attitudes. Despite these barriers, the interviews suggest that some girls do come to YTP to obtain non-traditional training. From their experiences in trying to obtain such training it has been possible to identify three processes at work within the programme which act to exclude them from non-traditional training; direct discrimination by staff who prevent access, attempts to channel girls into traditional areas by the imposition of double standards and sexual harrassment by male trainees in the training environment. There was evidence that staff attitudes may result in direct and explicit discouragement and in at least one of the schemes visited, there may have been actions or behaviours which would contravene the provisions of the sex discrimination legislation in that girls reported they had been told that courses were not open to them.

> They [the Careers Service] told me about all the different YTPs and what kind of jobs there were. I decided to come here. The Job Market says you can do anything on the form (training on offer by provider) and I wanted to do painting and decorating but I can't. [Community Workshop manager] doesn't allow wee girls into the wee lads' sections. (Female Trainee)

The experience of girls trying to obtain non-traditional training was well known throughout this centre, the effect of which was to discourage other girls from asking for non-traditional training. Thus, while a number of girls interviewed expressed an interest in non-traditional training, all were convinced that they would not be allowed to pursue such training.

Another, but no less effective, barrier to non-traditional training was the channeling of girls away from this by imposing a series of double standards for girls and boys. There was evidence to suggest that girls who wish to pursue a non-traditional training course had to prove a higher level of commitment and interest than boys and that their motives were legitimate. Thus for some staff, girls have to prove they are really interested in non-traditional training; that they do not "just want to chase the boys". There was also evidence that girls who wish to pursue non-traditional training are expected to prove that they are tougher and more resilient than other girls, tougher even than the boys. The requirement that girls project themselves as "one of the boys" is illustrated by the following, in which a male instructor compares and contrasts three girls he had trained in non-traditional areas, one in construction and two in motor vehicle repair.

> It's [motor vehicle repair] traditionally a man's area, so the boys tease them a bit. The girl in construction could hold her own. She was strong willed. She said [to him] "I hope you won't discriminate against me because I'm a girl". The two in motor vehicle repair are silly wee girls. They're a bit shy and retiring and the boys take the hand out of them.

The final factor is the hostile environment girls experience once in non-traditional training. A number of studies has documented the experiences of girls who have crossed gender boundaries in training in YTS, and they graphically illustrate the difficulties girls face (See for example

YWCA, 1986; Strafford, 1986; Cockburn, 1987). Such studies paint a picture of a training environment in which girls feel isolated, harassed and excluded by male trainees. For example, Strafford (1986) states that in the course of her fieldwork she never once heard a girl referred to by male trainees in terms other than those of sexual objectification. The study by the YWCA (1986) illustrates how sexual harrassment, obscene language, sexism and the display of female nude photographs are employed by boys in the training environment to exclude girls from, or isolate girls in, what they see as their "male territory".

A number of studies of working-class culture among the young has demonstrated the extent to which girls and boys inhabit different social worlds (See, for example, Jenkins, 1983; Coffield et al, 1986).

> Girls value one set of things (true love, marriage, caring, partnership) and boys value quite different things (the respect of other males, sexual freedom, female servicing). (Cockburn, 1986 p 31)

Coffield et al, (1986) argue that this results in the sexes viewing each other stereotypically, responding to each other in accordance with beliefs about the supposed characteristics of males and females, rather than as individuals. Girls are defined by boys in terms of their sexuality and such definitions are inevitably carried over into the workplace. At a time when gender identity is all important, the contradictions surrounding the incompatibility of being female in a male job, reinforced by the undermining or discrediting of this identity by male trainees, may quickly force girls to give up.

This seems particularly likely in the context of YTP as the interviews suggest that girls receive little support when they opt for nontraditional training with few concessions made for any lack of confidence or discomfort when faced with a male environment. In most cases, staff were simply unaware of the real difficulties girls experience in non-traditional training. In general, instructors and tutors who had experience of training young people in non-traditional areas identified few problems apart from "teasing", which was generally considered to be unimportant and to abate within a few days. The interviews with trainees, however, suggested that they are under no such illusions.

> I don't care what they [the girls] do. But the wee lads wouldn't like it if they came in. I know I wouldn't. They would get

> too much stick and the wee girls wouldn't like it either. (Male Trainee, Joinery)

> I wanted to do Painting and Decorating, but I wouldn't go into a class full of fellas. (Female Trainee, Catering)

> Girls would get stick, but if they can't take it there's no point going in. (Female Trainee, Office Practice)

Awareness that non-traditional training would mean having to cope with a hostile environment without support was widespread among girls and boys. This in itself may discourage girls from coming forward.

## Developing Equality of Opportunity in YTP

This Chapter has shown how, in the absence of an explicit governmental commitment to equality of opportunity for girls and boys in YTP, the attitudes and behaviour of scheme staff may actually reinforce pre-training experiences of young people, channelling girls and boys into gender-appropriate training and excluding girls from non-traditional training. What then are the levers for change?

Evidence from youth training measures in Great Britain suggests that overcoming gender segregation in training will not be an easy task. Despite the fact that equal opportunity for girls had been on the policy agenda of the MSC in relation to YOP and YTS, early responses, in the shape of simple affirmations of the Scheme's openness to all and later responses in the shape of special measures for girls (tagged on to mainstream provision), proved ineffective in breaking down gender segregation in any major way (Cockburn, 1987; YETRU, 1987). More recently, there has been a growing recognition within YTS that while special measures for girls such as single sex and reserved place schemes are important, there is a need to move towards a more comprehensive set of measures aimed at change in mainstream provision. In 1987, the MSC identified a number of steps directed at producing such change (MSC, 1987). These included the publication of an Equal Opportunities Code, a requirement that all organisations providing training demonstrate that they were taking active steps to promote equality of opportunity for girls and the setting up of a number of pilot local action plans involving local employers, careers advisors and schools.

Drawing from this British experience and from the research reported here, a detailed set of over 30 recommendations was drawn up for the case of YTP in Northern Ireland (See Montgomery and Davies, 1990). Given the attitudinal climate described in this Chapter, training for trainers may be the single most important of these recommendations, if action in this much misunderstood and complex area of social policy is to occur. YTP, however, is currently in the throes of an important change to greater employer involvement. Recent changes in the funding system introduced in April 1990 have been accompanied by changes in the structure of training. Young people will now receive an integrated two-year package of training and employment. There have also been changes in relation to access to the programme, so that providers are now able to recruit young people directly. In the absence of a strong equal opportunities policy, these changes may actually worsen the situation for girls who may be unwilling to risk taking up non-traditional training for this extended period and who may be even more unlikely to receive information on the full range of training options from employers than from scheme staff. Against this, however, the establishment of a Working Party by the Minister for the Economy in April 1990 to take forward the recommendations of the report, is an encouraging one.

Ultimately, the decision to take sex equality as a serious goal in the context of major changes in YTP and in the organisation of training policy in Northern Ireland as a whole will be a political one. What seems clear is that a real commitment to equality, if it is to be truly supportive of change has to be more than the paper commitment which is too often the starting and finishing point of action in this area.

## * Acknowledgement

The material from which this Chapter is drawn was gathered as part of a project funded jointly by the Equal Opportunities Commission for Northern Ireland and the Manpower Council.

# REFERENCES

BUSWELL C., (1988) "Flexible Workers for Flexible Firms" in A. Pollard,
G. Purvis and G. Walford (Eds), *Education, Training and the New Vocationalism: experience and policy*, Milton Keynes: Open University Press

COCKBURN C., (1986) "Sixteen: Sweet or Sorry?", *Marxism Today*, December

COCKBURN C., (1987) *Two-Track Training: Sex Inequalities and the YTS*,
Basingstoke: Macmillan

COFFIELD F., BORRILL C. and MARSHALL S., (1986) *Growing Up at the
Margins: Young Adults in the North-East*, Milton Keynes: Open University
Press

DEPARTMENT OF MANPOWER SERVICES/DEPARTMENT OF EDUCATION
FOR NORTHERN IRELAND, (1982) *A Comprehensive Youth Training Programme for 16/17 Year Olds in Northern Ireland*, Belfast:  DMS/DENI

DUFFY U. and McWHIRTER L., (1987) "Young People in Full-Time Work:
Evidence from the YTP Cohort Study", unpublished paper

FINN D., (1987) *Training Without Jobs: New Deals and Broken Promises*, Basingstoke:  Macmillan

FURLONG A., (1986) "Schools and Female Occupational Aspirations", *British
Journal of Sociology of Education*, 7(4), pp 367-377

GRIFFIN C., (1985) *Typical Girls?  Young Women from School to the Job
Market*, London:  Routledge and Kegan Paul

HOLLAND J., (1988) "Girls and Occupational Choice: in search of meanings",
in A. Pollard, J. Purvis and G. Walford (Eds), *Education, Training and the
New Vocationalism*, Milton Keynes: Open University Press

JENKINS R., (1983) *Lads, Citizens and Ordinary Kids*, London: Routledge and
Kegan Paul

McWHIRTER L., (nd) "Women in YTP", unpublished paper

MAGUIRE M. and ROPER S., (1990) "Vocational Training and Young People:
A Comparison of the YTP and the YTS 1982-87", in  M. Connolly and S.
Loughlin (Eds), *Public Policy in Northern Ireland: Adoption or Adaptation?*,
Belfast:  Policy Research Institute

MANPOWER SERVICES COMMISSION, (1981) *A New Training Initiative: a
consultative document*, May, Sheffield:  MSC

MANPOWER SERVICES COMMISSION, (1987) *Equal Opportunities for Young
Women in YTS:  Paper by YTS Programmes Branch*, unpublished paper YTB/
87/23

MONTGOMERY P. and DAVIES C., (1990) *Sex Equality in the Youth Training
Programme*, Belfast:  EOCNI/Manpower Council

REES G. and REES T. L., (1982) "Juvenile Unemployment and the State between
the Wars", in T. L. Rees and P. Atkinson (Eds), *Youth Unemployment and
State Intervention*, London:  Routledge and Kegan Paul

REES T., (1983) "Boys off the Street and Girls in the Home: Youth Unemployment and State Intervention in Northern Ireland", in R. Fiddy (Ed), *In Place
of Work: Policy and Provision for the Young Unemployed*, Lewes: Falmer
Press

REES T. L., (1984) "Reproducing Gender Inequality in the Labour Force: The
Role of the State", Paper 84/27e, Proceedings of the Standing Conference on
the Sociology of Further Education, Blagdon, Coombe Lodge

STAFFORD A., (1986) "Trying Work", PhD thesis, University of Edinburgh

WHYTE J., KILPATRICK R. and McILHENEY C., (1985) *Are They Being Served?
A Study of Young People in the Guaranteed Year of the Northern Ireland
YTP*, Belfast: NICER

YOUTH EMPLOYMENT AND TRAINING RESOURCE UNIT, (1987) *Young
Women and the YTS*, Birmingham: YETRU

YOUNG WOMEN'S CHRISTIAN ASSOCIATION, (1986) *Girls in Male Jobs?:
a research report*, Oxford: YWCA

# CHAPTER EIGHT


# RURAL WOMEN AND SOCIO-ECONOMIC DEVELOPMENT POLICIES: THE CASE OF SOUTH ARMAGH*

## AVILA KILMURRAY


## INTRODUCTION

South Armagh is known in the popular media as "Bandit Country", a title bestowed on it due to the area's high profile in the current Northern Ireland "Troubles". As such, the area may not seem the most likely focus for an examination of the needs and aspirations of rural women. However, in 1988-89 the Rural Action Project (Northern Ireland) undertook just such a study in cooperation with local women across the many communities that comprise South Armagh - women who would both question the media characterisation of their area and who were conscious of the need to highlight the issues facing rural dwellers.

South Armagh itself is a hilly, mountainous region, dotted through by a series of small lakes and rivers. Apart from a number of villages and hamlets, the population tends to be scattered in a dispersed settlement pattern across land that is poor in quality. In 1979 the majority of farms were between 20 and 35 acres, organised in a pattern of small fields of one to three acres (McGuinness, 1979). A combination of agricultural under-employment and a lack of alternative economic opportunities has resulted in high rates of registered unemployment and considerable dependence on social security benefits. Such economic problems are not recent in origin and elderly women still discuss the importance of female contributions to family incomes through work in the linen and lacemaking industries in the past. Women's earnings from such work were used for household necessities and survival itself. This responsibility was quietly assumed by generations of women, sometimes in cooperation with, and sometimes in spite of, their menfolk.

How far do such hard times persist? Jenny Beale is one writer who has put forward an optimistic view on women in rural Ireland.

> Talking to women about the differences between their own lives and those of their mothers and daughters, two main themes emerge. The first is the enormous change in living standards over just one generation, and how women's day-to-day work has been transformed by hot water, electricity and modern housing. The second theme concerns a change in women's perception of themselves; a noticeable shift towards a stronger sense of identity, towards women actively choosing their way of life rather than simply accepting a predestined role. (Beale 1986 p 1)

Beale's conclusions were based on a series of in-depth interviews with 27 women in the Republic. This Chapter is based on a study carried out by the Rural Action Project into the needs and aspirations of women in South Armagh (Kilmurray and Bradley, 1989). Data were generated in a number of ways, including a random sample survey of 296 women drawn from the electoral wards of Crossmaglen, Fathom, Forkhill, Creggan, Camlough and Newtownhamilton. This main sample was supplemented by a series of interviews with older women living in the area and by group discussions with 82 young people aged 14 to 18 attending local schools. Fieldwork was carried out in 1988. Fuller details on the methodology are contained in the main report (Kilmurray and Bradley, 1989). The study was carried out as part of the wider programme of the Rural Action Project, which was a four-year action-research programme funded under the European Commission Second Anti-Poverty Programme to identify and alleviate rural deprivation in South Armagh, West Fermanagh, Strabane and the Glens of Antrim.

## Women in South Armagh: Living Conditions

Certainly the standard of living and amenities in rural areas has improved considerably over the years as suggested by Beale (1986). Hot water, electricity and modern housing have been extended to communities in South Armagh, so that in the main survey only one elderly interviewee was living in a house without an electricity supply or mains water. That is not to say, however, that there was complete satisfaction with such services - problems of cost, irregularity and poor quality remain in relation to electricity and water. Nevertheless, the vast majority of women surveyed expressed themselves to be "satisfied" with most of the services, and were aware that the provision of these services was considerably better in South Armagh than in many other rural areas. This is particularly true of the housing stock. Some 80 per cent of the houses occupied by those interviewed were built after 1946 and 56 per cent were built after 1961. Such houses consequently had a reasonably high standard of amenities. Only five houses did not have either a fixed bath or shower, and four houses did not have an inside flush WC facility.

The 1981 Census data give more detailed information by ward on the number of households lacking basic amenities in this area. The Census showed over 80 homes in each of four of the six wards to be without a bath or shower.

Table 8.1:  Households by Amenities (Number in each Ward)

| Ward | No Bath/Shower | Outside WC Only |
|------|----------------|-----------------|
| Newtownhamilton | 89 | 16 |
| Camlough | 83 | 11 |
| Creggan | 77 | 13 |
| Crossmaglen | 45 | 8 |
| Fathom | 85 | 12 |
| Forkhill | 92 | 13 |
| Total | 471 | 73 |

Source:  1981 Census of Population, Northern Ireland

While South Armagh compares well with areas such as West Fermanagh, where one in every four houses is deemed to be unfit for habitation, figures such as these can hide problems. The Northern Ireland Housing Executive (NIHE) (West Region) has commented:

> Rural unfitness is difficult to see despite its extent. It is located everywhere but very often goes unnoticed. This is because it

> is hidden in the countryside, off main roads and from a dis-
> tance appears quaint and homely; rural dwellers take a particu-
> lar pride in keeping the external facade well decorated. This
> belies the fact that these houses are damp inside and lack basic
> amenities and are very cold in winter months.... (NIHE 1987,
> Section 2)

The fact that it tends to be the old and/or financially deprived who continue
to live in these houses has necessitated demands for a specific rural housing
policy to be agreed and resourced to allow rural housing conditions to be
improved. This problem is currently being considered, if not yet adequately resolved.

The survey found, however, that the service issues of most concern
were those related to accessibility. Both ease of communication and mobility
are crucial aspects of life in any rural community. It was these aspects
of life which Shaw (1979) proposed formed the basis of a Rural Deprivation Cycle (Figure 8.1) linking household deprivation on the one hand and
opportunity deprivation on the other.

Figure 8.1:  Rural Deprivation Cycle

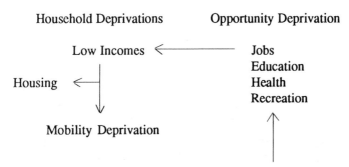

Transport Costs and Inaccessibility Rationing Opportunities

Source: Shaw, 1979 p 184

Another commentator on rural deprivation, Cooper (1978) makes a
similar point about the importance of mobility and access:

> ...It is the relationship between constraint on access and deprivation which makes the question of mobility crucial to any consideration of poverty in rural areas ...Policies of national and local government which affect access and mobility therefore warrant examination.... (Cooper, 1978 p 5)

Such a cycle of deprivation is most likely to affect specific groups in rural areas such as the elderly, the young, and women (who may be deprived, for instance, of a car when the husband/partner is working away from home). The 1981 Census showed that between a third and half of households in South Armagh had no car (Table 8.2).

Table 8.2:  Households by Number of Cars, South Armagh, 1981, %

| Wards | No car | 1 car | 2 cars | 3+ cars |
| --- | --- | --- | --- | --- |
| Newtownhamilton | 41 | 47 | 10 | 2 |
| Camlough | 31 | 54 | 8 | 1 |
| Creggan | 41 | 49 | 8 | 1 |
| Crossmaglen | 52 | 42 | 5 | 1 |
| Fathom | 32 | 53 | 12 | 3 |
| Forkhill | 45 | 46 | 8 | 1 |

Source:  1981 Census of Population, Northern Ireland

Unusually for a rural area, the proportion of households without a car in South Armagh is higher than the Northern Ireland average. There are also fewer households than average with two cars. This would suggest a considerable degree of deprivation given that car ownership is generally regarded as a necessity rather than a luxury in rural circumstances.

Where there is a car available to the household, this does not, of course, guarantee women's access to it. As many as 76 per cent of the women in the survey lived in households with either one or no car; and nearly half of the women interviewed had no driving licence (Table 8.3). This rose to over three-quarters among women who were pensioners.

Table 8.3:   Women's Possession of a Driving Licence,
South Armagh, 1988

|  | All | | Pensioners | |
|  | N | % | N | % |
|---|---|---|---|---|
| Driving licence | 169 | 57 | 9 | 16 |
| No licence | 124 | 42 | 45 | 79 |
| No response | 3 | 1 | 3 | 5 |
| Base | 296 | 100 | 57 | 100 |

Clearly a high proportion of women are dependent on either public transport or on the availability of other family members or neighbours to offer them transport. Public transport was used by 72 of the 124 women without driving licences on a regular basis. Those who did not use public transport cited infrequency of services, long distances from their houses to the nearest bus stop, and no bus service to the required destination as the main reasons for this. The importance of public transport to rural women and the low level of current provision meant that improvement to public transport was the change most frequently called for by rural women when they were asked about all services in their area. Thus, 75 per cent wanted to see a more frequent bus service, while smaller proportions wanted more bus shelters; more frequent bus stops; less expensive fares and the provision of community buses.

Present government policies (for example, deregulation of the bus system in Northern Ireland) seem unlikely to promote widespread expansion of public transport in rural areas and indeed restriction of current levels is a distinct possibility. There is no evidence, either, of awareness at governmental level of the extent of mobility deprivation among rural women (and to a lesser extent men). One woman with no access to a car described her situation succinctly in these terms:

> Nearest local shop 2-3 miles. Public transport, irregular. No school bus for school which is three and a half to four miles away.

That mobility deprivation has a huge impact on rural women's quality of life is not difficult to see from this woman's brief description of her situation.

Even those women in rural areas who do have access to a car face the time pressures of regularly travelling distances - particularly if they have children to get to and from school and other activities or are caring for dependent adults.  Half of those women caring for elderly relatives in the South Armagh survey mentioned difficulty of access to services and/ or the time spent in travelling to and from the cared-for person's home. As one woman pointed out, ''[It] takes up a lot of time - [I] travel a distance of 26 miles per day''.  Rural carers thus face particularly strong constraints on participation in employment or training and, not surprisingly, two-thirds of the female carers interviewed said their caring role had prevented them from considering employment or training opportunities.

Women with young children were also very conscious of the possible impact of distance and social isolation, despite the obvious many advantages for children of growing up in a rural area.

> Children can be isolated - [you] have to put an effort into their
> activities...Having to transport them in and out to services,
> school, pictures, etc.

Indeed the distance issue, the lack of local facilities and social isolation were the most important concerns for women bringing up children in South Armagh.

Overall, this study and Census data certainly confirm Beale's (1986) assertion that the standard of life has improved for women in rural areas, so too do the comments of many rural women in South Armagh themselves.  But such improvements must be seen both in the context of the grinding poverty of previous years and in relation to the standard and quality of life attainable in non-rural areas.  It remains the case that rural people and rural women in particular face considerable levels of mobility deprivation.  Mobility and accessibility deprivation may well have sharpened over recent years with the gradual withdrawal of services and facilities from many rural communities.  Added to this is the official assumption that virtually all rural dwellers have ready access to private transport.  As the above discussion has shown, this is clearly not the case for women in South Armagh, a situation that limits both their opportunities for personal development and their capability for involvement outside the home.

## Women in South Armagh:   Economic Activity

Transport and childcare were two of the issues which featured highly among women who were eager to obtain employment outside the home. In terms of childcare, South Armagh has an even higher proportion of its population under the age of 16 than does Northern Ireland as a whole (33 per cent compared to an average of 30 per cent), yet childcare facilities in the area were restricted to Mother and Toddler groups and to a number of nursery schools. The majority of women who were employed either had their children minded by relatives or paid a childminder. The other main options seemed to be either to work part-time or else to wait until the children were old enough to look after themselves after school. That 32 per cent of the employed women in the survey were working less than 21 hours per week, and 21 per cent less than 16 hours per week, may well be linked to this. Jobs that were both local and that consisted of hours that fitted in with childcare responsibilities, however, were not easy to find in a rural area characterised by high unemployment. In the event, a sizeable number of women were employed in their own home vicinity (45 per cent), while some of those employed in the nearest large town - Newry - complained about the "very low wages and very long distance to travel...".

The service sector was a major source of employment for women in South Armagh. The public service sector was particularly noteworthy, with at least 54 per cent of those interviewed working in this sector. Public spending cut-backs and Government privatisation policies may thus have serious implications for women in the area. Few alternative employment options for women in this area were apparent.

Unemployment, and the lack of employment opportunities in the region, was a major preoccupation with the vast majority of the women interviewed, and was clearly identified as the main reason why the area was considered to be disadvantaged. However, much of the concern the women expressed was focused on the needs of men and the young, leaving the impression that employment opportunities for married women may well be a matter of secondary interest to them when balanced against the haemorrhage of emigration from South Armagh. It may be that many women had internalised the perception that their prime role should be seen as that of home-based wife and mother, despite the generations of women who had worked outside the home in an attempt to make ends meet. Nevertheless some women certainly did highlight the neglect of women's unemployment in the area: "There is no work for the local women. Women are forgotten about in rural areas". And most women regarded employment for women, even those with young children, in a positive light.

When asked specifically whether women with young children should work outside the home if work was available, 47 per cent of such women said "yes"; 30 per cent felt that it depended on family circumstances; and only 11 per cent said "no". When compared with the responses of female pensioners, a generational difference in attitude can be seen. Thirty-eight per cent of older women thought that women with young children should stay at home. Moving to the views of yet another generation - the 82 secondary school children interviewed - interestingly, there was a even greater divergence of opinion between girls and boys than between older and younger women. Seventy-four per cent of girls felt that women with children should work outside the home, while 42 per cent of boys were clear in their feelings that these women should remain at home.

If there has been a change in attitudes across the generations towards women working there would seem to be less movement in the area of job selection and segregation. While there was a certain limited range of variation in the "ideal occupation" choice of those young women who intended to stay on at school to sit for higher examinations, the job choices of the girls who intended to leave school at an earlier age showed a dispiritingly high level of stereotyped job selection. The choice of childcare, secretarial and clerical work, nursing, hairdressing, and so on, was a clear echo of the jobs of women already employed in the region. Such selection may, of course, have simply been a realistic assessment of the job options available, but it was no less depressing for all that. If the reaction of the young women themselves is to be believed, little faith can be placed in the potential of current youth training provision to alter the situation. Indeed, if anything, there was a clear belief expressed that the general bias of the facilities available was towards boys (See Montgomery, Chapter Seven). Training was also a matter of concern to women in the survey. Faced with the suggestion of a Women's Training Workshop, almost all the women who were not working (112 out of 119) thought that this would be a useful facility in the South Armagh area. In addition to this, over half (54 per cent) of all the women interviewed said that they would personally be interested in attending courses or training of some kind. Preferred options for further training tended to reflect the type of occupation available in the area, and related to clerical, caring, crafts and catering work. Some more venturesome souls, however, noted in addition to this the need for assertiveness, DIY and farming skills.

Training for farm-based economic activity was also mentioned by a number of women who themselves were members of the farming community. Considering this point in the context of the Republic of Ireland, O'Hara (1987) has drawn attention to the need for in-service training for farm women, since most will have entered farming on marriage and will have had no prior experience of this area of work. South Armagh women argued that attendance at relevant and accessible courses would enhance professional status, recognition and self-confidence of farm women.

Of the 25 women living on farms who answered the questionnaire, most felt that their role had changed over the years. The introduction of machinery even on small farms was identified as a crucial element in this changing role. Opinions varied about the impact. One woman stated that the update of farm machinery meant she could be more involved; others, on the contrary, thought that "machinery has taken over, women don't do as much". Nevertheless, older women in particular were quick to point out that the introduction of labour-saving machinery had reduced the virtual "slavery" of farm women - a welcome development, and long overdue. In years gone by, what small farms had lost by having extremely limited capital available, they had made up through the investment of family labour.

Small farmers are still dependent on the contribution made by women to the farm household income through regular off-farm employment. Buttel and Gillespie (1984) examined the relationship between rural women's on-farm and off-farm employment. Farm size was an important variable in determining family labour allocation; as was the life-cycle of the farm household, the level of skill and education, and the availability of job opportunities. Relating this analysis to small farms it was felt that they had little alternative but to either accept a low standard of living or to work off the farm to supplement farm incomes. This conclusion can be applied to the prevailing situation in South Armagh, although limited alternative employment can obviously limit the off-farm income available. While individual women may have a clear perception of the importance of their contribution to the family income and/or farm, the actual named owner and recognised decision-maker in the farming community still tends to be male. Few women in the South Armagh study had land in their own name - unless they were widowed - although in some cases land was in the joint names of the woman and her partner. In only one case did a woman clearly fall into the category of a "woman farmer" as identified by Gasson (1981). She portrayed three role types: the farm housewife who is a home-centred person, only helping on the farm in emergencies or by undertaking book work, answering the telephone, running errands, etc; the working farm housewife who spends part of every day working manually on the farm, but with a clear division of the farm labour between herself and her male partner; women farmers who have a clearly defined responsibility in relation to the farm and may well be farming either in partnership with their husband or alone. In the majority of cases, women either fulfilled the role of farm housewife, or else were engaged in off-farm employment while at the same time carrying out some farm tasks that were complementary to the farmer's own role. A supportive role, performing secretarial work for example, caring for humans and animals, transporting people and objects, often went unacknowledged and was taken for granted in a rural community otherwise acutely aware of the struggle for survival. Women in South Armagh spoke about how marginal they felt in the farm decision-making process, and how the long hours and hard work of combining farm duties, household tasks and, in some cases, off-farm employment, meant that they were more restricted than many of their urban counterparts. Yet the challenge of "keeping the name on the land" is still, it would seem, a major consideration for as many women as men, and given the limited economic options in South Armagh, pluriactivity - involving all family members drawing income from a number of sources - would often appear to be the only feasible strategy for survival.

In economic terms, women in South Armagh would thus seem to be caught between the demands of finding employment in order to help make ends meet both in the village and on the farm, while at the same time being acutely aware of the impact of competition for scarce jobs in the local area. The inherent danger in this situation is that women can become prey to low pay, poor conditions and insecure employment. But then, as the women themselves pointed out - what choice is there?

### Development Policies for Rural Women

Rural women in South Armagh are increasingly aware both of their own predicament and the economic difficulties facing their communities. Two-thirds of the women in the study regarded South Armagh as either disadvantaged or very disadvantaged. Specific aspects of disadvantage were listed as unemployment and lack of employment opportunities; isolation and poor accessibility; lack of facilities; poor transport; and the presence of the army and impact of the "Troubles". What is clearly required to address the range of issues highlighted is a strategy of regeneration for the whole region - but a strategy that will be informed, not only by the totality of need, but also by the needs of particular sections of the rural community. For this approach to be effectively achieved, the needs of the rural poor, and of groups such as rural women, must be clearly articulated.

Nearly two-thirds of the women in the survey considered investment in developing tourism in the area a priority. In addition women discussed the need to support self-help enterprises; cottage industries; improved local facilities; and the attraction of potential employers to the area. Agricultural diversification was also discussed, although the combination of lack of capital and information resulted in many being unsure of the feasibility of this option. What emerged, in short, was a view that defiantly refuted outside perceptions of South Armagh as a peripheral rural area doomed to terminal economic decline. The alternative scenario articulated by the women of South Armagh presented the prospect of an integrated plan for the area which would both increase employment opportunities and the possibility for realising a pluriactivity economy.

The training and employment of women, including older women, is an essential part of rural development given the fact that such women will clearly be remaining in their area, and thus have much to contribute to both the community and to their own families. Women's roles and attitudes are changing, but Gasson's (1981) caution may still be well founded:

> Women's liberation is likely to mean fewer women content with traditional, subordinate roles in farming, more determined to become farmers. These women risk opposition on all sides. Society expects women to have jobs nowadays, it is true, but not in occupations which threaten the status of men. On a farm a woman may undertake "suitable" work but not "masculine" tasks like marketing livestock, ploughing or driving a combine. For women to do these things undermines the traditional authority of men. (Gasson, 1981 p 19)

Gasson's view may usefully be extended to rural women outside those in the farming community, and it underlines the need for training and support for those women who are seeking to develop outside the stereotyped areas of employment.

In an International Symposium on Women in Rural Areas, the training and continuing education of rural women was much discussed (Council of Europe, 1989). The Symposium also addressed strategies for enhancing the economic independence of women in the countryside, and the legal and social position of women in the countryside. Of particular interest was the emphasis on the need for childcare facilities; support for economic initiatives undertaken by women; an assessment of the input and value of unpaid work by women; and the need to improve rural infrastructure if women are to achieve a higher overall level of economic independence. Apart from the monitoring of unpaid work, most of these issues had already been identified as important by women in the South Armagh study.

There was less awareness, however, of the many essential aspects raised by the Council of Europe discussions on the legal position of rural women. In addition to the recommendation that all appropriate measures should be taken to improve the position of rural women under social security and labour law, it was also suggested that the company or partnership rights of women on farms needed to be protected. Creating a structured framework to increase the participation of women in public life and in decision-making in rural areas as both local and regional levels was also identified as a priority.

The commitment of necessary resources for the development of areas outside the designated District Towns in Northern Ireland is not at present an accepted part of environmental and economic policy. Yet without such a commitment, the very real danger is that the survival of traditional rural communities will be bought with the condemnation of many rural dwellers to a low standard of living. It is important to ensure that this prospect is averted through the thorough examination of other options, such as the development of locally-based new technology industries, or the underpinning of pluriactivity with appropriate social security benefits and agricultural grants. What both community-based and official policies also have to recognise is the commitment and the contribution that women can make to community development. Women's contribution to the revitalisation of a region much in need of such commitments can only be increased by an investment in the individual development of rural women themselves.

The Rural Action Project study in South Armagh has emphasised that women are the mainstay not only of rural households, but also of rural communities, in areas suffering severe deprivation. Whilst women's main consideration in an area such as South Armagh is the development of a society which will offer a viable future for all their children, such women not only have commitment to the area, but have ideas about economic regeneration and the part they can play in it. It is women's ideas as well as other elements which must now be considerations in any integrated development plan for rural areas such as South Armagh.

## * Acknowledgment

The material from which this Chapter is drawn was gathered as part of a project carried out by the Rural Action Project with financial assistance from the EOCNI, entitled *Rural Women in South Armagh: Needs and Aspirations*, carried out by this author and Carmel Bradley.

# REFERENCES

BEALE J., (1986) *Women in Ireland: Voice of Change*, Dublin:   Gill and Macmillan

BUTTEL F. and GILLESPIE G., (1984) "The Sexual Division of Farm Household Labour:  An Exploratory Study of the Structure of On-Farm and Off-Farm Labour Allocation among Farm Men and Women", *Rural Sociology*, 49 (2)

COOPER S., (1978) *Rural Poverty in the United Kingdom*, London:   Policy Studies Institute

COUNCIL OF EUROPE, (1989) *The Conclusions and Declarations of a Colloquium on the European Campaign for the Countryside; Women in Rural Areas Symposium*, Strasbourg:  Council of Europe

GASSON R., (1981) "Roles of Women in Farms:  A Pilot Study", *Journal of Argicultural Economics*, 32 (1)

KILMURRAY A. and BRADLEY C., (1989) *Rural Women in South Armagh: Needs and Aspirations*, Londonderry:  Rural Action Project (NI)

McGUINNESS P., (1979) "Application by the South Armagh Farmers" Association for Inclusion of Lands in the Disadvantaged Areas (Northern Ireland Scheme).  Submission to the Permanent Secretary, Department of Agriculture, Belfast

NORTHERN IRELAND CENSUS OF POPULATION, (1981) Belfast:  HMSO

NORTHERN IRELAND HOUSING EXECUTIVE, (West Region) (1987) *The Roslea Study: A Study into Rural Housing Unfitness in West Region*, Omagh:  NIHE

O'HARA P., (1987) "Farmwomen: Concerns and Issues of an Undervalued Workforce", paper presented at the UCD Women's Studies Forum, Dublin

SHAW M., (1979) "Rural Deprivation and Social Planning: An Overview", in M. Shaw (Ed), *Rural Deprivation and Planning*, Norwich:  University of East Anglia, Geo Abstracts Ltd

# CHAPTER NINE

# REFORMING THE AGENDA

## CELIA DAVIES

The contributors to this volume have much in common. From their different starting points of trying to explore and explain developments in social policy and of trying to campaign for change through trade unions and voluntary agencies of one kind and another, they have all developed a continuing concern for inequalities between the sexes. These inequalities, which seem to be built in both to the design and operation of a wide range of different policies, are rarely overt and on the surface. In the case of rural development, for example, and in the case of youth training, it is a matter of policy development which has either ignored women altogether, or has assumed (erroneously) that the needs of women and men are the same. In the case of childcare, it is a matter not of what is done, but rather of what is not done (or even conceived of as potentially viable or worthy of consideration).

Nor, again as the contributors make plain, does the academic study of these areas always offer a corrective. Gender inequalities, as the Introduction has suggested, have been lower on the list of priorities than other matters, and the extent of the challenge provided by work that has been carried out from the standpoint of women has still not fully been confronted. Eileen Evason offers more than a hint of this when she quotes Gillian Pascall, commenting that we need to ask questions about the structures of the academic disciplines which have left women out, and when she concludes that it is change in conceptualisation that is most important (Chapter Four, p 62). In Monica McWilliams' Chapter too, it is clear that she is herself confronting a range of ideas about women's employment that are so taken for granted that it is hard to clear the ground, let alone to pose and consider more relevant hypotheses.

To read these Chapters in quick succession is to be struck by the centrality of the authors' concern with women's paid employment. This is present not only in those Chapters that deal directly with jobs, pay and training, it is a theme too in the Chapters on rural women and on poverty. What is made abundantly clear is that women's access to paid employment - to the main route to an income of one's own - however fast this is growing, is not on the same terms as men's access. Women are not integrated in the labour market in the same way. The sexual segregation of work by sector and by occupation, the part-time ghetto, low pay and poor prospects, these are all key features of paid employment for the majority. The jobs that men do can be, and are, organised as if there were no other obligations to take into account and no work of the unpaid variety to be done; the jobs that women do have to be organised around domestic, childcare and other obligations, so that:

> (A)s women continue to fit in and be fitted in with employ-
> ment that revolves around their families' needs, they could
> find their access to pensions, maternity leave and sick pay
> further restricted. (McWilliams, Chapter Two, p 35)

Because paid employment and unpaid employment are so deeply inter-twined for women, and because women's options are so narrowed by current arrangements, a book on social policy and women has also to be a book on economic policy on women.

## Dependency and the New Agenda

The single most important contribution of students of social policy in relation to women in recent years has been their insistent focus on women and dependency. Women's dependency was a design feature of the post-war welfare state measures in Great Britain and was transposed to Northern Ireland intact. Along with a dependency on the male breadwinner who would accrue rights from employment, went women's side of the bargain, unpaid labour in support of that breadwinner and of other family members. Women's increased participation in paid employment, and, as recent statistics for Northern Ireland suggest, smaller family size, have effected considerable alterations in women's lives. Yet the observation that there has been no consequent revolution in the economic roles of men and women (Joshi, 1989 p 157), is amply borne out by the contributors to this volume. It will be the tensions between dependency in the old form and the new demands of economic restructuring which will shape and govern much of the development in this sphere for women in the 1990s. What then of the preferred policy framework? There is a considerable amount of consensus among contributors not only about the need to break the model of the male breadwinner and female dependent but also about the ways in which this could be done. Monica McWilliams puts in a particular plea for change to the incentive structure that keeps the wives of unemployed men out of the labour market and for support structures that recognise the links which women need to forge between home and work. Bronagh Hinds devotes her whole attention to childcare policy as a crucial plank in a policy that will recognise and support women's employment, as well as one that will recognise children's rights to stimulating and developmentally appropriate services. Hazel Morrissey looks to a new specification of the rights of all who are employed, as exemplified in the European Social Charter and in various Draft Directives. Eileen Evason offers the longest list - measures to combat low pay and to take account of and credit unpaid work as well as a reshaping of the social security system. Her suggestion of a "principle of equal concern" to cover the contingencies of women's lives as well as those of "men and their wives" offers, in one concise phrase, a basis on which change in social security could be built.

What the contributors do not always put in so many words, however, is that it is the link between opportunities for employment of different kinds and access to social security benefits which needs to be revised in any new social policy provision. And such a revision raises fundamental questions about both economic and social goals.

The Organisation for Economic Cooperation and Development (OECD), as part of its continuing series of investigations of the economic outlook for its member countries, has recently provided an important comment on this. The postwar economic goals of full employment and a range of social and welfare protections, it argues, were simple. The aspiration was that by tying benefit entitlements to employment-based insurance contributions for a "breadwinner", such a breadwinner could be somehow independent of the State even when caught by the contingencies of unemployment, disability and old age. Brief periods of income support would be needed in face of exceptional contingencies, small groups would fall through the net, but in the main, a man would support his wife and children through his wage. The problem, as the OECD puts it, is that the basis for this settlement has now been eroded by factors such as unemployment, increasing use of non-standard patterns of employment, family structure changes, and a "quest for independence". These changes weaken the direct links between employment and social protection, and have not yet been "matched by corresponding entitlements to social protection" (OECD 1989, p 8).

Early reponses to the new situation, rationing jobs in various ways, and then engaging in programmes of job creation, are now seen by the OECD as deadends. It notes that a new policy strand is emerging, moving towards more "active" societies.

> This approach welcomes - rather than resists - the entry of new groups into the labour market. It recognises the demand for participation in economic and social life which is increasingly voiced by most groups in the population, and does not seek to resist the expression of this demand through a growth in aggregate labour force participation. Instead, the underlying goal is to enhance the effective productivity of the population as a whole by drawing on previously-unused talents, and harnessing them in a more effective and comprehensive division of labour...The aim thus is not to "define away" unemployment by assigning those seeking work to some other status, but rather to recognise that realisation of the full human potential of the population involves the employment not only of the unemployed, but of all those who wish to participate - whether working full-time, part-time, or in casual employment. (OECD, 1989 p 9)

This approach implies diverting resources devoted to "passive income maintenance", to widened training opportunities linked with income support, and funding "guided forms of training and employment which will preserve income security entitlements while encouraging labour force participation". It also means not just accepting full-time employment and the permanent lifetime career as a norm, but recognising and facilitating "non-standard employment", linking this to social protections in such a way that it will be in the interests of many of those not currently "active" economically to participate in income generation. This relates to older people who might otherwise be retired and to young people who might plan a different mix of study, employment and training. It also, of course, has considerable potential for women.

While references to women are not prominent in the OECD discussion, the approach outlined is consistent with improvements for women and does specifically mention that in broadening the tax base (a key goal for an "active" society), both the revision of tax structures so as to remove any discouragement of participation by men and women and the broadening of childcare provisions will be necessary. Some of this is distinctly reminiscent of the themes put forward in the mid 1980s and reiterated more recently by Charles Handy in his vision of "flexi-lives" for all rather than the full-time, life-long male career (Handy 1984, 1989).

What, then, is the likelihood of such thinking developing either directly in Northern Ireland social policy or permeating more indirectly from changes in Great Britain?

## The Dynamics of Endless Postponement

The observations made in the Chapters of this book, and the suggestions for change, are not entirely new. They form part of a body of work which has been growing in the United Kingdom for at least a decade, and which has echoes in discussions in other settings, among these, Australia (Sharp and Broomhill, 1988) and the USA (Bose and Spitze, 1987). The processes by which women's interests are denied, and issues of relevance for women are kept off the agenda of discussion are many-fold, and building on the work of Magrit Eichler (1988), I would highlight four.

Failure to problematise issues of women's needs and implications of policies for women is supported first by two closely related processes, widespread androcentricity and misplaced universalism. By androcentricity is meant that the yardstick of thinking in relation to social and economic policies is a male yardstick, and that the constant point of reference is male. Misplaced universalism means using terms that are apparently abstract and applicable to all, but in practice apply only to a dominant group.

A good example where both of these are apparent is in the OECD document referred to earlier. Having noted that the significant decline in the employment: population ratio for men has been more than offset by women entering the labour force, the authors go on to comment:

> **This decline** has clearly been in part a response to a decline in employment opportunities: countries with a low unemployment rate show the lowest declines (and even increases in recent years). Hence there is now considerable variation amongst OECD countries in the extent to which their **people** of working age are engaged in paid employment. **People** have withdrawn from the labour force least in countries with low unemployment rates, although the tendency of men to retire early has also been influenced by other factors. (OECD 1989, p 33) (emphasis added)

First, there is androcentricity: the two processes alluded to (decline in male employment, rise in female employment) are conflated into one. It is the decline (for men) not the rise (for women) which is deemed worthy of further comment. Then, there are the two universalistic reference to "people". On the first usage, the term seems to be wellfounded. There is indeed variation between people in the degree to which they are engaged in paid employment, variation between people of the two sexes being one such. The second reference, however, makes clear that this is not what is meant. To talk of the contexts in which "people" have withdrawn least, is to revert to a discussion of the matter of the ratio decline, the matter which refers only to men. The overall result therefore, in a document that paradoxically contains much discussion of women's employment and unemployment, deprioritises women, and helps to postpone consideration of issues of relevance to them. What the issues are in relation to women, and what, if anything, the relation between the trends for the two sexes is, are questions that go unanswered. Some of the same myopic vision is apparent in discussions of women's employment in Northern Ireland as we will see in the next Section.

Secondly, there is the question of double standards. In her Chapter, Pamela Montgomery has given clear examples of double standards thinking at work amongst those who select girls and boys for youth training. One of the most wellknown and frequently cited examples of double standards in academic conceptualisation in the field of work is the use of "job models" and "gender models" respectively in attempting to explain men's and women's commitment to work (Feldberg and Glenn, 1979). A job model attributes attitudes to work to the circumstances of the work, its nature, conditions and so on, whereas a gender model atributes attitudes (women's presumed lesser commitment to work, for example), to their sex. A gender model serves, therefore, to confirm the stereotype. Starting from a belief in the essential differences between men and women, it frames questions and designs a study in such a way as not to allow the possibility of similarity to enter. A recent review of a wide range of evidence, however, has concluded that when men and women in a similar situation are compared, and when the model applied is the same, then it is the similarity, not the difference in response that is notable (Dex, 1988 p 80-81). Monica McWilliams' in her Chapter, has to steer a difficult path around double standards. This is apparent as she contests not so much double standards in the shape of fullblown gender models which have informed enquiry into women's employment in Northern Ireland but rather double standards in the shape of assumptions about women's lesser participation (both compared with men and compared with women elsewhere) which seem so natural and taken for granted that even to pose the question or to do the study would be superfluous. Androcentricity, misplaced universalism and double standards have been powerful factors in shaping the framework of policy and research and together they contribute to the dynamics of postponement. A fourth factor stemming from the framing of basic questions in these ways, is that conceptualisations and the accounting processes to which they give rise can help to render women's activities and indeed women themselves less visible. This, of course, was the message of Eileen Evason's Chapter on poverty in this volume. But other contributors have commented for example on the concept of "economically inactive" and the category of "keeping house" (McWilliams), as well as on the convention of excluding from the PAYE scheme and hence from an "earnings survey", those who have non-standard employment and those with very low earnings (Morrissey). The way that women's occupations are "bunched" into a small number of categories where men's are more evenly spread, the dearth of information on contracts other than full-time, the problem of the registered unemployed and the discouraged worker are further issues that come to mind from the considerable literature now dealing with forms of sexism in official statistics (Oakley and Oakley, 1979; Hunt, 1980; Nissel, 1980). What is ostensibly gender-blind can in practise be gender-biased (cf Davies, 1989a) in this regard, and women, less likely to be on the agenda in the first place, can find their contributions further minimised by the conventions of data collection and presentation.

Alongside these important issues of the framing of socioeconomic policy and of the debates around such policy, we need to consider the impact of the legislation designed directly to address gender inequalities in the employment field, namely the legislation on sex discrimination and equal pay. Patricia Maxwell, in this volume, has traced the limitations of recent developments in relation to equal pay, highlighting a lack of commitment on the part of government, and a morass of complexity in the operation of the legislation, not helped by the actions of the judiciary.

Looked at more broadly, the equality legislation originating in the 1970s has been of undoubted benefit to numbers of individual women. It has also served an important function of legitimating debate, and has generated both attitude and behavioural change which should not be underestimated. It has not, however, proved effective in changing overall patterns of occupational segregation, low pay and unpaid labour, or in addressing the issue of dependency that is raised in this volume. This is not surprising. Students from a wide range of disciplines, including economics, law, history, social policy, anthropology and sociology are now arguing that the concept of equality built into that legislation is a limited and limiting one. The limitations stem from abstracting women from the net of obligations that governs their lives, and from insisting on a strict identity of treatment with men, which, in such a context, is clearly an overly simple response. I have discussed this in more detail elsewhere, drawing on the work of Jewson and Mason (1986) and linking it to a model of liberalism which has contradictory implications for women in the current social structure (Davies, 1989b). I have also argued that since the mid 1970s, when equal pay and sex discrimination legislation came into effect, virtually all the thinking about women, men and employment has been thinking that is oriented to the particular notion of equality built into that legislation. This 1970s equality model, with its uncritical acceptance that justice must always be blind to factors such as gender, and race, has been powerfully analysed in terms of producing outcomes of formal rather than substantive equality (Gregory, 1987). And it has also has not only acted as a brake on further policy development, but has also produced a set of reactions from women themselves, which include frustration, confusion and guilt (Davies, 1989b, 1990). Heather Joshi has commented in this regard that:

> Sex-blind treatment appeals to women's self-respect, and is fine for those who have successfully seized new opportunities in education and the labour market, but as long as equal treatment extends only to paid work, it does not give proper recognition to the contribution and need of most women. (Joshi, 1989 p 157)

The predominant concept of equality is thus a further factor contributing to the dynamics of postponement.

Finally, there is the question of context, and of the balance of forces for and against the complete reforming of social and economic policy which the consideration of this volume as a whole suggests. This brings us to the issue of the specific setting of Northern Ireland and the opportunities, or lack of them, that it presents as far as change in the social and economic policy agenda is concerned.

## The Northern Ireland Context

The predominant concern in relation to economic and social policy in Northern Ireland in the last decade and more has been concern with inequalities between the Catholic and Protestant "communities" (that is, between Catholic men and Protestant men), not concern with inequalities between Catholic women and Protestant women or concern with inequalities between women and men in general. The record number of amendments to the Fair Employment Bill as it progressed through the parliamentary process in 1989, together, of course with the action of paramilitary forces, helped to ensure that British "news" about Northern Ireland continued to be news about the two religious communities. It also helped to ensure that the energies of politicians, civil servants and community leaders were similarly channelled. Some commentators have been specific in laying a large part of the blame for inaction and confusion on religious discrimination at the door of the Northern Ireland civil service (McCormack and O'Hara, 1990). Others, Osborne and Cormack (1989), for example, as was noted in the Introduction, have further suggested that energy has been devoted specifically to ensure that there is no "read-across" from action on inequality in relation to religion to action on inequality in relation to gender, race or disability. This then, is to present a pessimistic picture as far as action for women is concerned.

Nor can one fail to be at least somewhat pessimistic when examining the plans for economic regeneration emanating from the Northern Ireland Department of Economic Development (DED). "Pathfinder" was a project that captured much energy and enthusiasm in the quest to build a stronger economy. But its six Task Forces, established to map out the route for the future, gave very little consideration either to the current or to the future contribution of women, save in the one case of targetting women as an underrepresented group in the area of new business start-ups (DED 1987).

Then there is the matter of training policy. The new Training and Employment Agency, launched in April of this year, has taken over the functions of ten previous bodies, including the DED itself in the employment and training sphere. One central aim is to give more direction and purpose to a previously fragmented policy area; another is to ensure the more effective involvement of industry in relation to training. The role and function statements of the new Agency, while targetting "young people and the unemployed, including the disabled", make no specific mention of women at all (DED, 1989: para 14iii). Also, notwithstanding the scope that was present in the Draft Order-in-Council establishing the new arrangements, the structure of a central Board and sectoral and representative Advisory Bodies, is specifically designed to be industry-led, leaving little scope for a routine input from those with special knowledge of the needs of different target groups. How far, therefore, this new structure will be able to accommodate the growing evidence of women's training needs in Northern Ireland (See McCorry, 1988; Montgomery, Chapter Seven), and how far it will encourage and nurture initiatives of existing agencies which are starting to target women (the Local Enterprise Development Unit's current "Enterprising Northern Ireland" campaign, for example), remains to be seen.

The most recent policy document from DED, "Competing in the 1990s" (See Davies, 1990), is resolutely universal in its references to "the workforce", "young people" and "the unemployed" and it acknowledges the importance of eliminating discrimination on a number of grounds, gender among them. The only point where women get a specific mention, however, is in the Appendix. Here, in the context of a discussion about the difficulties of bringing the unemployment rate down, women's rising numbers in the workforce are noted. It is hard to conclude anything from this other than that women present at the least, a difficulty, at the most, an embarassment.

There is, as the quotation Bronagh Hinds provides from a document from the Industrial Development Board (IDB) suggests, sometimes a recognition that there are negative attitudes to women's employment among employers (Hinds, Chapter Six p 98). But few would guess from most of the official policy statements on the economy in Northern Ireland that women are already approaching 50 per cent of employees in employment, and that some (See Morrissey, Chapter Three), predict that women will be in a majority among Northern Ireland's employees by the turn of the century. Of course, there are some women entrepreneurs, some women running manufacturing businesses and some women involved in export-led services. But the majority of the jobs that women do are servicing and enabling jobs, and are frequently jobs in the public sector. The growth in the service sector in the last two decades has not been seen as something to be proud of, in the way that a similar expansion in heavy industry would have been lauded. The tacit assumption seems to be that these are not "real jobs", that they are the dirty linen of overall employment - something to be covered over, certainly not to be discussed in public!

The trade union movement, through the mechanism of the Irish Congress of Trade Unions (ICTU) and through individual unions, has done much to criticise the overall economic strategy of the Northern Ireland Office and to present an alternative economic strategy. It has not shrunk from putting forward highly controversial ideas, like integration of the economies in the North and South of Ireland (See, for example Moriarty and Morrissey, 1988) - but it has not, as yet at any rate, made the full integration of women into the economy a high profile topic. A case can be put against all this pessimism, however. In the first place, developments in the fair employment field may well turn out to be an asset rather than a liability. A number of business firms and public sector organisations, anticipating the legislation, have seen fit to appoint equal opportunity managers, and an Equal Opportunity Managers' Group formed in the summer of 1989, had a membership in excess of 20 almost immediately. Prior to this, equal opportunity managers had been a rarity in Northern Ireland. Since the remit of such managers usually extends also to equal opportunities for women, and since the monitoring information required by the new Fair Employment Commission is routinely required for men and women separately, the prospects, both for information and action, are good. Furthermore, while one can debate the pros and cons of the separation of equality agencies, it is worth noting that the Equal Opportunities Commission for Northern Ireland itself argued against an integrated approach (EOCNI, 1988), and is already vigorously campaigning in those areas where its counterpart now has greater power.

Secondly, the last word has by no means yet been said about the future shape of the economic regeneration debate. Major uncertainties relate here to Northern Ireland's future level of integration with the British economy, with the economy of the Republic of Ireland and with the economies of both Western and Eastern Europe. New directions in official policy prompted by external developments or by internal developments, by women in the trade union movement, for example, are not inconceivable. Several of the contributors to this volume hold out strong hope for development in some economic and social policies relevant for women via the actions of the European Community. Although we should take heed of the implicit warning in Patricia Maxwell's Chapter that change which is imposed on a reluctant member state can be effectively undermined in a whole number of ways, the Directives currently under discussion and the provisions of the Social Charter do come close to setting out a new, and more woman-friendly basis for labour market participation.

In looking to possible futures, much might be said of the parties involved, including the British Government and opposition, the Northern Ireland civil servants and politicians and the framework in which these operate. The women's movement is important here, and there is no doubt that, notwithstanding divisions between organised groups of women, women's demands are more complex and more nuanced than they were a decade ago. It is also the case now, as it was not before, that women, some of them clearly alert to the kinds of issues raised in this book, have gained positions within major institutions and lobbying agencies in Northern Ireland and this too is part of a new power equation. An important indication of the present balance of forces may soon emerge with the availability of European Structural Funds for initiatives in training. There is an explicit aim to target women and to devise programmes of relevance to women's needs. To date, Northern Ireland's history in provision in this area has been dismal.

Whatever the future, no-one can dispute that women's lives have changed markedly in recent decades. Women still in mid-life in Northern Ireland will have entered the labour market at a time before equal pay and sex discrimination legislation came on the scene, whereas women entering the labour market today can take this policy framework entirely for granted. Whether born of economic restructuring, of European pressure, of pressure from the organised women's movement, or all of these, it is not inconceivable that both generations of women will see the kinds of changes advocated in this book. The outline, and indeed, the detail of many of the changes in social and economic policy that are necessary to aid women are already clear. All that remains is for them to take their place on the agenda.

# REFERENCES

BOSE C. and SPITZE G., (1987) *Ingredients for Women's Employment Policy*, Albany, NY: State University of New York Press

DAVIES C., (1989a) "Gender Blindness and Genderbias: Problems of Sexism in Official Statistics", paper presented at PPRU Seminar, Stormont, Belfast, July (unpublished)

DAVIES C., (1989b) "Workplace Action Programmes for Equality for Women: An Orthodoxy Examined", in C. Hussey (Ed), *Equal Opportunities for Men and Women in Higher Education* (conference report), Dublin: University College Dublin

DAVIES C., (1990) "Equality, Fairness and the Reality of Women's Employment", inaugural lecture, 22 May 1990, University of Ulster at Coleraine

DEPARTMENT OF ECONOMIC DEVELOPMENT, (1987) *Building a Stronger Economy: The Pathfinder Process*, Belfast: DED

DEPARTMENT OF ECONOMIC DEVELOPMENT, (1989) *Training and Employment Services in Northern Ireland*, Belfast: HMSO

DEPARTMENT OF ECONOMIC DEVELOPMENT, (1990) *Northern Ireland: Competing in the 1990s: The Key to Growth*, Belfast: DED

DEX S., (1988) *Women's Attitudes towards Work*, London: Macmillan

EICHLER M., (1988) *Nonsexist Research Methods*, Boston Mass: Allen and Unwin

EQUAL OPPORTUNITIES COMMISSION FOR NORTHERN IRELAND, (1986) *Response to the Consultative Document "Equality of Opportunity in Employment in Northern Ireland: Future Strategy Options"*, (Department of Economic Development), Belfast: EOCNI

FELDBERG R. and GLENN E., (1979) "Male and Female: Job versus Gender Models in the Sociology of Work", *Social Problems*, 26(5)

GREGORY J., (1987) *Sex, Race and the Law*, London: Sage

HANDY C., (1984) *The Future of Work*, Oxford: Robertson

HANDY C., (1989) *The Age of Unreason*, London: Hutchinson

HUNT A., (1980) "Some Gaps and Problems Arising from Government Statistics on Women at Work", Manchester: Equal Opportunities Commission *Research Bulletin 4*

JOSHI H., (1989) "The Changing Form of Women's Economic Dependency" in H. Joshi (Ed), *The Changing Population of Britain*, Oxford: Basil Blackwell

McCORMACK V. and O'HARA J., (1990) *Enduring Inequality: Religious Discrimination in Employment in Northern Ireland*, London: Liberty, NCCL

McCORRY M., (1988) *Women and the Need for Training*, Belfast: Women's Education Project

MORIARTY T. and MORRISSEY M., (1988) *The Economies in Ireland*, Belfast: MSF

OECD, (1989) *Employment Outlook*, Paris: OECD

OAKLEY A. and OAKLEY R., (1979) "Sexism in Official Statistics", in J. Irvine et al, (Eds), *Demystifying Social Statistics*, London: Pluto Press

OSBORNE R. and CORMACK R., (1989) "Fair Employment: Towards Reform in Northern Ireland", *Policy and Politics*, 17(4)

NISSEL M., (1980) "Women in Government Statistics: Basic Concepts and Assumptions", Manchester: Equal Opoprtunities Commission *Research Bulletin 4*

SHARP R. and BROOMHILL R., (1988) *Shortchanged: Women and Economic Policies*, Sydney: Allen and Unwin

# INDEX